C000175679

PORTRAIT OF THE
Pines Express

Stephen Austin

First published 1998

ISBN 0 7110 2624 6

All rights reserved. No part of this book may be
reproduced or transmitted in any form or by any
means, electronic or mechanical, including
photocopying, recording or by any information storage
and retrieval system, without permission from the
Publisher in writing.

© Stephen Austin 1998

Published by Ian Allan Publishing

an imprint of Ian Allan Publishing Ltd, Terminal House,
Station Approach, Shepperton, Surrey TW17 8AS.

Printed by Ian Allan Printing Ltd, Riverdene Business
Park, Molesey Road, Hersham, Surrey KT12 4RG.

Code: 9811/B1

Front cover:
Class 4F No 44102 pilots No 34043 *Combe Martin* on the
southbound 'Pines Express' at Masbury in 1962.
J. G. Dowling/Colour Rail

Back cover:
Birmingham New Street. The northbound 'Pines' running into
Platform 7 from the Birmingham West Suburban Line, past
No 5 Signalbox, on 8 April 1961. Engine No 45590
Travencore. M. Mensing

Title page:
Bath station, now named Green Park, in its latter days. Just
before 10 o'clock on the morning of 29 August 1964, the
9.30am from Bristol, due to reverse and depart at 9.55 to
Bournemouth, is running in; engine No 73037 is a BR
Standard Class 5. In the other platform the 10.10am to Bristol
is ready to leave. *D. M. Aldred*

Above:
Stanier 4-6-0 Class 5 No 44851, has just cleared Wickwar
station and is heading north with the up 'Pines Express' on
9 May 1953. *IAL*

Right:
The scene at Oxford shed on 1 November 1965. Brush diesel
No D1691 is ready to take over the northbound 'Pines', with
the number already on the roller blinds. The other engines are
pannier tank No 3677, 'Black Five' No 45038 and No 6998
Burton Agnes Hall (later preserved by the Great Western
Society). *A. D. McIntyre*

Contents

Acknowledgements

The line and colour of this portrait is derived from the railway company timetables and other papers held in the Public Record Office, and from the reports in *Railway Magazine* and *Railway World*. Illustrations are drawn from the publisher's collection, and Colin Boocock, John Gomersall, John Haddock, Rex Kennedy, Michael Mensing, David Rapson and Dick Riley have helped with photographs. I am also grateful to the Bournemouth Libraries, Mr and Mrs Oram and Chris Austin. And just as no train would run without a vast amount of technical support, this essay would not have appeared without the support of my sister, Janet Price.

Selected Bibliography

The Somerset & Dorset Railway,	Robin Atthill
Liverpool: A People's History,	Peter Aughton
Jubilees of the LMS,	John F. Clay
Discovering Inland Lancashire,	R. and M. Freetly
LMS Engine Sheds,	C. Hawkins and G. Reeve
The LMS Coach,	D. Jenkinson and R. Essery
The Somerset & Dorset in the Sixties,	Ivo Peters
Gradients of the British Main Line Railways,	The Railway Publishing Co
Portrait of the Solent,	Barry Shurlock
Class 47 Diesels,	A. Taylor, W. Thorley and T. Hill
Midland Steam,	W. A. Tuplin
Rail Centres: Oxford,	Lawrence Waters
David & Charles Regional History of the Railways:	
Vol 2; Southern England,	H. P. White
Vol 7; The West Midlands,	R. Christiansen
Vol 10; The North West,	G. O. Holt

Note *Pre-decimal currency*
Prior to decimalisation in 1971, the pound sterling was divided into 20 shillings (s), each of which was subdivided into 12 pence (d). A guinea was one pound and a shilling. References to money, for fares etc, in the text, use the conventions of pre-decimal currency where appropriate.

Above:
The junction of the main and Styal lines at Wilmslow. On 12 June 1950 the up 'Mancunian', hauled by 'Royal Scot' No 46168 *The Girl Guide*, has been diverted via Styal. *T. Lewis*

Introduction

Portrait of the Pines Express

On the south coast of England the ancient limestone rock of the Jurassic period defies the elements to form the Isle of Wight and the Isle of Purbeck. Between these two masses lie more recent strata, the Oligocene sandstones, and the soil which results from them is too light and dry for most English plants to flourish. In the hinterland of Bournemouth the characteristic growth is of heathers, gorse and pine trees.

If you were a child living in Manchester, geology probably meant nothing much to you, except as one of those school subjects bearing no relation to real life. However, you would be aware that you did not see pine trees in Manchester. When, after a long day's travelling, you had found your boarding house and at last were released for the first exploration of the holiday, there were pine trees close at hand and they were your first stop. The soaring height of them, the susurration of wind in their tops, the carpet of needles they laid beneath them, the resinous smell of them that filled the air; all made you feel, with the absorption of the moment which we can only experience while we are children, that you had been transported to another world. It was entirely appropriate that the train, the magic carpet, that brought you there should be called the 'Pines Express'.

In tracing out this portrait of the 'Pines' I have had to grapple with its special characteristics. It was not remarkable as a train; at no time distinguished by anything special in the way of motive power or rolling stock. It was not, in general, noted for speed; indeed, over much of the distance it was an express in name only. Because it did not run from London it was ignored by the commentators of the day, so this picture has to be assembled from what fragments are to be found. Photographers, too, preferred to take their pictures out in the country rather than in the backyards of industry, and were inclined to overlook such everyday sights as shunting and empty stock working. Thus the record is very patchy on what was really special about the 'Pines': the peculiar routes it took.

British railways were very complicated, nowhere more than in the area of Birmingham. New Street station lay in the centre of the north-south Midland Railway main line, the east-west London & North Western route and the Grand Junction line from the north-west, and by a network of link lines, trains to

and from any route could, and did, pass through it in either direction, or bypass it altogether. The 'Pines' did all these and, for a period, used the rival Great Western line through Snow Hill station. Not only were regular trains scheduled on different paths from day to day, but the controllers and signalmen were adept at switching them around at short notice in the event of a holdup or breakdown. Details were not published and of course did not matter to passengers on their way through. Consequently, any readable account must be somewhat simplified, so if these pages say that something happened in Birmingham, it should be taken as something that *probably* happened in Birmingham.

There is a convention on the railways which describes trains as travelling either 'up' (towards London) or 'down' (away from London); these directions were defined for every piece of railway, so that the staff were clear about which direction was which. In the case of a cross-country run the designations were somewhat arbitrary and you would at some point pass through a reversal. Thus, when proceeding from Park Lane Junction to Castle Bromwich Junction, on the outskirts of Birmingham, a 'Pines' would change from being an up train to a down train. To avoid confusion on this point, I refer to it as southbound (sb) or northbound (nb).

Above:
Evening Star in the period when she was based at Oxford, on shed on 4 June 1963. Behind her is 2-6-2T No 6144, stored out of use.
N. E. Preedy

5

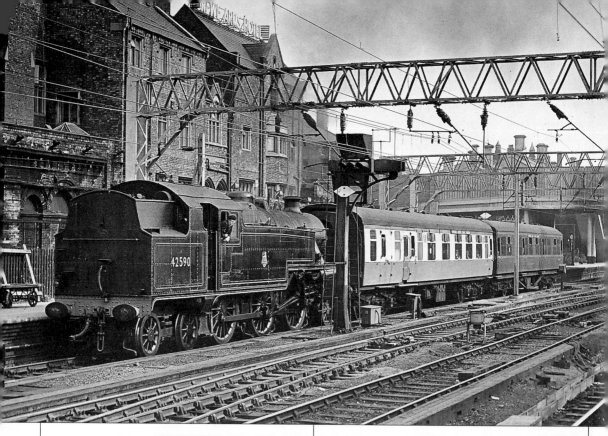

Above:
Shunting through coaches at Crewe station, north end. The destination boards are not quite legible, but the first two words are Plymouth and Bristol, so they could be the Glasgow coaches being taken off the 8am Plymouth-Liverpool.
T. Lewis

Above:
No 44687, the last LMS 'Black Five' built in 1951, had roller bearing axles, British Caprotti valve motion, double exhaust and a higher running plate to facilitate the cleaning which might have taken place. She is seen in Platform 7 in New Street, with the 9.25am Bournemouth-Liverpool on 10 September 1960. This engine and sister No 44686 spent their lives at Longsight. *M. Mensing*

The Invention of Bournemouth

Portrait of the Pines Express

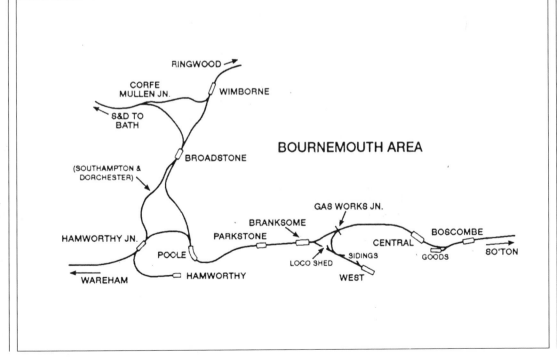

The bleak cliff-top land between the small ports of Christchurch and Poole, backed by meagre heath and facing the dangerous sea, was broken only by a gully where a stream so insignificant that it had no name but was just called The Bourne trickled into the sea. Here in the year 1810 Louis Tregonwell had the eccentric notion of building himself a house. Word began to spread about the tranquillity, mild climate and cheap land and, at first gradually, a resort grew. In 1841 the resident population was 905, then up it went: 1851 — 1,330; 1871 — 5,900; 1881 — 16,900; 1891 — 27,900; 1901 — 60,000; 1911 — 78,700; 1931 — 116,800; 1961 — 154,000. These figures alone do not include the equally rapidly rising populations of Poole and Christchurch and only indirectly represent the rise in numbers of holidaymakers.

The developers built a pier, planted pine trees — three million of them according to local legend — and placed a pine atop the town's emblem, over the motto 'Pulchritudo Et Salubritas'. Although it would not have occurred to the early settlers, the cliff became an advantage in later years when the motor car arrived, for it enabled the beach to be separated from motor traffic and thus kept quiet for the elderly as well as safe for children. The gullies down which peaty streams trickled became sheltered gardens, essential for a year-round resort. The hoteliers put great emphasis on this latter aspect and were active in encouraging winter visitors to keep the tills ringing. In this they had the co-operation of the railway companies.

Although the railways' contribution to the growth of Bournemouth is undeniable, they did not create it; they actually approached it slowly and reluctantly. Until 1859 the Southampton & Dorchester Railway (known as 'Castleman's Corkscrew' from its sinuous course and its energetic chairman) thought it was adequately served by a branch to Hamworthy, on the far side of Poole. This first railway connection opened on 1 June 1847, and became part of the London & South Western Railway a year later. Another branch from Ringwood to

Christchurch opened on 13 November 1862, and in a leisurely way advanced to a terminus outside Bournemouth on the Holdenhurst road, which finally came into use on 14 March 1870. Meanwhile, the Somerset & Dorset Railway began running from Burnham-on-Sea to Wimborne on 31 August 1863 and sponsored the Poole & Bournemouth Railway, whose completion from Poole to Bournemouth West on 15 June 1874 enabled its trains to run into Bournemouth over a connection, built by the LSWR, from Broadstone Junction to Poole.

Not until 1885 did work start on a link from the East to the West stations. It was built around the northern edge of the town and its line shows us the extent of the built-up area at that time. It came into use on 30 May 1886, at the same time as a cut-off line from Lymington Junction to Christchurch, which finally put Bournemouth on the main line and relegated the Southampton & Dorchester to secondary status. Even then, trains passing through from east to west had to reverse at Bournemouth West and Broadstone until 1893.

Each of these developments brought a new surge of house-building. As at many resorts, the railway fed the growth of the town, which in turn fed the traffic of the railway.

A through service from the industrial Midlands to the south coast was first tried by the Great Western and South Eastern Railways; it ran from Birkenhead to Dover and Hastings. It started on 1 July 1863, but was given up three years later. In 1874 the Somerset & Dorset completed its extension from Evercreech Junction to Bath, joining up with the Midland Railway line from Birmingham. From the outset two of the four daily passenger trains each way included Birmingham coaches, worked forward by the Midland, which was then negotiating a take-over of the S&D jointly with the LSWR.

The timings were:

	s/bound	s/bound	n/bound	n/bound
Birmingham	d 9.5am	d 2.20pm	a 3.35pm	a 4.55pm
Bournemouth	a 3.25pm	a 9.40pm	d 7.25am	d 10.15am

These commenced on 20 July 1874, were reduced to one train a day during the winter, and resumed in May 1875. The times of 6hr 20min southbound and 6hr 40min northbound were not impressive.

The lease of the S&D, completed the following year, created a Joint Committee to manage the former company. It gave the Midland a system spanning England from Carlisle to the south coast, although only gradually did it begin to exploit this coverage. In early years, of course, the low speeds made very long journeys seem unattractive ordeals to the public. One such was attempted in 1889 when the Midland/LSWR partnership offered a through train from Bradford to Plymouth, an odyssey of 383 miles which was perhaps before its time and was short-lived.

In those days Manchester was one of the greatest cities of the world. It may be associated in a lot of snobbish minds with clog-wearing, impoverished mill-slaves, but it was also a centre of free thought and radical ideas and had a record of contribution to the arts and sciences far superior to, for instance, London. At the forefront of technology, it was the city served by the first wholly artificial waterway and the first main-line railway. By the mid-19th century it had already grown so that it and surrounding towns such as Salford, Oldham, Ashton and Stockport were fusing into one gigantic built-up area. But if the railway facilitated this conurbation, it also brought the means for the inhabitants to escape and enjoy that other great Victorian invention, the seaside holiday.

Left:
Bournemouth's pier was one of the few to be rebuilt in the late 20th century. The concrete sections were completed in 1981. This view was taken on 23 September 1997. *Author*

Above:
Gateway to the country and the seaside:
Liverpool Lime Street. *S. Lovell*

Manchester and Liverpool received a through service to the south coast in 1904, in the form of the London & North Western and London Brighton & South Coast 'Sunny South Express' to Brighton and Eastbourne. The Midland was then running through coaches to Bournemouth from Bradford and Leeds, Newcastle and York, and to Bristol from Liverpool and Manchester. But what stung it into further action was the news that, for the 1910 summer timetable, those old rivals the Great Western and London & South Western were putting on a restaurant car express between Birkenhead and Bournemouth. And to rub it in, this had a portion from Manchester London Road, via Crewe and Market Drayton, to join the main train at Wellington.

The response was ready on 1 October 1910 and was a joint venture between the Midland and the London & North Western Railway, whose lines were used from Manchester London Road and Liverpool Lime Street to Birmingham New Street. One can speculate on why, in those competitive days, the Midland should join forces with the firm which had just allowed the GWR to lift business from under its nose, when it could have used its own tracks and those of the Cheshire Lines to reach its own Manchester Central and Liverpool Central stations. However, railway politics were more complex than the simple battleground often portrayed. Relations between the Midland and the Great Central were not

easy, although they were partners in the Cheshire Lines, and the latter was also collaborating with the Great Western on northeast to southwest services. No matter how belligerent the stance adopted for public show, rival companies were co-operating more and more through the medium of the Railway Clearing House, a process which would doubtless have continued had it not been for the war and Government control. To go from Manchester over the Pennines to Derby and back over to Birmingham would have been possible but would never have enticed any patrons off the North Western via Crewe, so it made sense to work together on this one.

The new train, not then blessed with a name (the Midland never named trains nor, with two exceptions, engines), was announced in the October 1910 timetable thus:

SPECIAL NOTICES
New Express Service
Manchester London Road   & Liverpool Lime Street   and Bournemouth
via Crewe and Birmingham

Right:
Not all housing in industrial towns is like this, but a lot of it is. This is Stockport, at some time after 1959, when the overhead wire equipment had been fitted on the viaduct. Of the near houses, only three have television aerials and one appears to be on the telephone. Nearly all have their original sash windows. *IAL*

At Crewe, Manchester and Liverpool portions joined into one train. It went on through Stafford and Wolverhampton to Birmingham New Street, where the black LNWR engine was changed for a crimson Midland one. Southwards through Gloucester, it ran on directly to Bath by means of the triangular junction at Mangotsfield; there the Midland engine was replaced by a blue one of the Somerset & Dorset for the run to Bournemouth. On paper, it was nonstop from Bath to Poole.

On the way north, the two parts separated at Birmingham. Additional stops at Bailey Gate and Blandford on the S&D were for the purpose of passing other trains.

An oddity of the working arrangement was that it always passed through Birmingham New Street station in the same direction, from west to east. The southbound train arrived from Wolverhampton and departed turning right from Curzon Street Grand Junction to St Andrew's Junction on the Midland Railway main line via Camp Hill to Kings Norton. The northbound train arrived on the Birmingham West Suburban line from Kings Norton through Selly Oak, and departed turning left to the Grand Junction main line through Bescot to Bushbury Junction. Since 1885 most Midland expresses bound for Gloucester passed westwards through New Street and used the Birmingham West Suburban line, so at its inception this train was a pursuer of unusual routes.

Left:
A Somerset & Dorset express conveying three through coaches from the Midland, offering decidedly superior comfort to the three S&D coaches behind them. The engine is No 70, a standard Midland 4-4-0 supplied in 1914, which became BR No 40322 and was scrapped about 1955. *LGRP*

Left:
At Bath Queen Square station in the early 1920s. A typically dressed schoolboy admires No 15, one of the first 4-4-0s built for the S&D in 1891. The poster cases on the far wall belong to both Southern and LMS, and above them is an enamel advertisement for the Midland Hotel. *LGRP*

Advertised times were as follows:

Liverpool	d 9.45am	a 4.45
Manchester	d 10.0	a 4.2
Stockport	d 10.9	a 3.50
Crewe	d 10.45	a 3.47
Birmingham	a 11.53, d 12.3pm	a 2.10, d 2.17 and 2.20
Cheltenham	a 1.0, d 1.2	a 1.0, d 1.5
Gloucester	a 1.13, d 1.18	a 12.45, d 12.50pm
Bath	a 2.8, d 2.13	a 11.47, d 11.55
Blandford	-	d 10.22
Bailey Gate	-	d 10.10
Poole	a 3.54	d 9.53
Parkstone	-	d 9.47
Bournemouth	a 4.7	d 9.40am

The Crewe departure time of 10.45 was a piece of fiction which was kept up for many years; in fact the train arrived at 10.41 and left at 10.49. Arrival at Birmingham was just 1min after another express came in from the Derby line. It included carriages from Heysham, Manchester, Bradford, Leeds and York. It paused for only three minutes, and the timetable contained a 'Note: the 9.45am from Liverpool and the 10am from Manchester do not connect with the 11.55am Birmingham to Bristol.' It did, however, drop off the York coach, which was attached to the Bournemouth express. A restaurant car was also attached, to work through to Bournemouth.

On the northbound run, in one of those tantalisingly obscure details of the lost art of railway working, the

11

Above:
This undated view, probably late 1920s, shows the northbound 'Pines', with clerestory and elliptical roof coaches, passing Templecombe No 2 Junction; the photographer is standing in front of the box. Behind the train the connecting line rises to the upper station. On the left is the S&D engine shed. *Real Photographs*

Left:
A poster for Bournemouth brightens Manchester Piccadilly. This view was taken in 1968, a year after the through service ceased. *K. P. Lawrence*

Above:
A view from Edge Hill No 2 signalbox in the 1920s. A North Wales express, hauled by a Midland Compound, comes up the main line from Lime Street. Between the engine's steam and the signal are parts of the original 1836 buildings. *Real Photographs*

restaurant car only appeared at Gloucester, to run to Birmingham. It could have been a matter of load limits on the S&D, for the train also had through coaches to York, Leeds and Bradford. They were detached at Birmingham and went forward at 2.25 on the 12.20pm Bristol-Leeds/Bradford.

	s/bound	n/bound
York	d 7.30am	a 7.55pm
Leeds	-	a 5.32pm
Bradford	-	a 5.58pm

Bradford portions did not go round through Leeds to the Midland's Forster Square terminus, but used a connection, brought into use the previous year, from Middlestown Junction to Thornhill on the Lancashire & Yorkshire Railway, south of Dewsbury, and thence into Bradford Exchange. In these arrangements we see the Midland working with both the LNWR and the LYR, and a ticket interavailability scheme operated on a number of routes where they were not in direct competition.

Several other connections were offered:

	s/bound	n/bound
Blackpool Central	d 7.50am	a 6.25
Preston	d 8.50	a 5.27
Wigan	d 9.15	a 4.57
Warrington	d 9.36	a 4.38
Birkenhead Woodside	d 9.20	a 5.0
Chester	d 9.53	a 4.25
Huddersfield	d 9.20	a 5.40
Oldham Clegg Street	d 9.20	a 5.11pm
Blandford	a 4.11pm	
Parkstone	a 4.34	
Branksome	a 4.39	d 9.33am

Another connection was the Midland & South Western Junction Railway's 1.12pm Cheltenham-Southampton, arriving at 5.22, and the 7.25am from Southampton, which was not much of a connection as it kept you waiting at Cheltenham from 11.15 to one o'clock. Broadly, the pre-'Pines' conformed to the idea of the 40mph express, common at the time, although it is notable that the times were not improved upon until the mid-1960s. Indeed, from Birmingham to Manchester the LNWR 4-4-0 engine with its half-dozen wooden-bodied coaches made the same pace that British Rail achieved with the aid of 4,500hp diesel engines 90 years later. This is not to disparage the efforts of engineers in the interim; but even 'High-Tech' enthusiasts must recognise that given the facts of geography, one cannot always go on developing one corridor of transport no matter how much money is poured into it, and such expenditure may not always be to the benefit of the customer or the community at large.

In those days the fare from Manchester to Bournemouth was 36s 6d first single, 19s 10d third single, 68s 1d first return, 39s 8d third return. A horse could go for 70s 6d, a dog for 5s, children under three free, children three to 12 half fare. You could have your luggage delivered to your residence or hotel for 6d per item.

A short-lived addition, tried in the summer of 1922, was a through coach from Manchester to Swanage, detached at Broadstone and taken on by the LSWR. Otherwise the pre-'Pines' continued largely unchanged, except for the period from 1917 to 1919 when the railways were controlled by the Government and it was suspended. On 1 January 1923 it was inherited by the new London, Midland & Scottish Railway.

Below:
The 'Pines Express climbs the 1 in 50 crossing Prestleigh Viaduct between Evercreech junction and Shepton Mallet hauled by 40569 and 73047 on 6 April 1957. *C. P. Boocock*

'Pines Express', 1927-1962

Portrait of the Pines Express

The General Strike of 1926 was a terrible shock to the railways, but in the case of the LMS it could be argued that it had one virtue: it caused that hitherto unmanageable body (the largest joint-stock company in the world to date) to pull itself together and start moving in a co-ordinated manner. Its new Chairman, Sir Josiah Stamp, was a director of the Bank of England and initiated a regime that could best be described as 'businesslike'. You could not imagine the LMS being so enthusiastic as to allow its engineers to spend company time demonstrating television on moving trains, as the LNER did, or being so feudal as to issue an order like this one in the Great Western timetable of the period:

'A representation having been made to the Railway that their Servants should be required to use every care to avoid running over Packs of Hounds, which during the Hunting Season, may cross the Line, all Servants of the Railway are hereby enjoined to use every care consistent with a due regard being paid to the proper working of the Line and Trains'.

Below:
At Bath station in about 1928, as the 'Pines' prepares to leave for Bournemouth. The then new 4-4-0 No 46 was the last engine supplied to the Joint Committee; she became No 635 and lasted until 1958. The driver is leaning on the Whitaker tablet catcher. Note that everyone on the station is wearing a hat. *Real Photographs*

26 September 1927		
Manchester LR	d 10.0am	a 4.50
Stockport	d 10.9	a 4.39
Liverpool LS	d 9.40	a 5.20
Crewe	d 10.45	a 3.56
Birmingham NS	d 12.6pm	a 2.45
Cheltenham Spa	a 1.14	d 1.39
Gloucester	a 1.28	d 1.23
Bath	a 2.31	d 12.30pm
Blandford	a 4.3	d 10.59
Poole	a 4.28	d 10.33
Parkstone	a 4.35	d 10.26
Bournemouth W	a 4.44	d 10.20am
Ludgershall	a 3.34	d 11.22
Andover Jn	a 3.48	d 11.5
Southampton W	a 4.36	d 10.12
Southampton T	a 4.46	d 10.5
(Commencing 7 May 1928)		
Bradford FS	d 7.38am TWTh	a 6.35 WThF
Leeds Wellington	d 8.15 TWTh	a 6.0 WThF
Sheffield	d 9.30 TWTh	a 5.2 WThF
Chesterfield	d 9.57 TWTh	a 4.38pm WThF

It did indulge in some investment in marketing, although with an eye on the pennies it persuaded the LNER to go shares in a holiday guide book, and took some cautious steps to brighten up its image.

At this time the only named train on the LMS was the 'Irish Mail', and that was not so much a name as a description. In early 1927 came an announcement that, from 11 July, the 10am Euston-Glasgow and Glasgow-Euston services were to be named the 'Royal Scot'. When this first foray proved not too painful but actually quite enjoyable, the summer was spent thinking up more names and in the autumn timetable, to begin on 26 September, there were 16 of them, including the 'Pines Express'. The naming could be regarded as the swan-song of T. C. Jeffries, who retired in June from the post of Head of the Publicity and Advertising Department; he had been Chief of Advertising for the Midland Railway since 1903. Alternatively, it could have been an innovation by his successor, G. H. Loftus Allen. It has been claimed that the 'Pines' was the formal adoption of a nickname bestowed by passengers.

Below:
The northbound 'Pines' at Masbury summit in 1936, a winter formation hauled by LMS 4-4-0 No 630. The building in the distance survived until the 1960s. *LGRP*

Above:
A Bristol-Sheffield express of the 1930s ascending
the Lickey Incline. 'Black Five' No 5285 and Midland
Class 2 No 508, with only eight on, both have ample
steam, but seem to be leaving the work to the
banker. *H. Gordon Tidey*

July 1929		
Manchester LR	d 10am	a 4.50 SX 5.5 SO
Stockport	d 10.9	a 4.36 SX 4.52 SO
Liverpool LS	d 9.40	a 5.23
Crewe	d 10.45	a 3.56 SX 4.15 SO
Wolverhampton HL	d 11.40	-
Birmingham NS	d 12.8pm TWTh	a 2.45 SX
Cheltenham Spa	a 1.13	d 1.39
Gloucester	-	d 1.23
Bath	a 2.25	d 12.30pm
Sandford	a 4.51	-
Poole	a 4.24	d 10.32
Parkstone	-	d 10.26
Bournemouth W	a 4.36	d 10.20
Ludgershall	a 3.46	d 11.23
Andover Jn	a 4.0	d 11.6
Southampton W	a 4.49	d 10.18
Southampton T	a 4.58	d 10.10am

Bournemouth in 1927 had settled into the character
it was to keep for the rest of the century. Its
preoccupations were the weather, traffic problems and
the prospects for local employment.

There was being advertised 'the last opportunity
of acquiring Land on the Coast in Bournemouth', the
Branksome Dene estate, so the resort was now
complete and any further expansion would have to
take place inland. You could buy a house for around
£1,500 (pricey for those days) and a lady's coat cost
3-5 guineas.

One thing that stands out in the literature of the
time is the railways' total preoccupation with London.
Whether they are to be congratulated on helping to
compress the population into that dreary corner of
England and thus preserving more pleasant
countryside, or condemned for forcing into central
London masses of transient travellers who had no need
to be there, is open to debate. Beyond question is that
services radiating from London were first in the queue
for every penny of investment, and the railway press
seldom if ever mentioned any others. Of 66 trains
blessed with names up until World War 2, 49 ran from
London, 10 within Scotland and seven elsewhere,
including the 'Pines'. The entry of the latter into this
elite list is a measure of how hard Bournemouth had
been pushing the LMS for improved services. The local

press was pleased to announce that, for the summer service beginning on Monday 11 July, through trains from the north were being restored and improved, with some additions. Noted were:

Saturday 7.33am from Birmingham and 6.12am from Derby.
Friday and Saturday from Nottingham arriving 4.14pm.
10am from Manchester/9.40am from Liverpool.
10.40am from Lincoln via Nottingham, Leicester, Birmingham.
6.25pm from Bath with connections from Birmingham and beyond.
Saturday 9.30am to Birmingham, Leicester, Nottingham, Lincoln.
9.45am to Birmingham, Derby, Leicester, Lincoln, Leeds, Bradford.
10.20am to Crewe, Manchester, Liverpool.
Monday and Saturday 10.50am to Birmingham etc.
1.35pm to Birmingham and Derby.
5pm to Bristol and Birmingham.

All these used the West station. To attract business from the town centre the LMS continued to use the Midland's office at 284 Old Christchurch Road and placed booking agencies with the firms of Cook's and Pickford's.

Below:
Southampton Terminus station in 1923.
Beyond it is the station hotel, where the Cunard family had a suite permanently reserved, and beyond that is Canute Road.
Real Photographs

In the summer of 1927, what was to become the 'Pines Express' was still the 1910 version with the addition of a through coach from Liverpool to Southampton. It still had the prestigious departure time of 10am from Manchester London Road. It stopped at Stockport Edgeley, from 10.10 to 10.12, and Crewe, 10.41-10.49. Here the Liverpool portion, which left Lime Street at 9.40 and reached Crewe at 10.31, was attached. What happened after that depended on what day it was. On Tuesdays, Wednesdays and Thursdays it ran up the Grand Junction main line through Bescot and Aston to Birmingham New Street (11.57-12.6). Here the engine was replaced by a fresh one at the other end of the train, and it departed via the curve onto the Midland line at Camp Hill, to head south to Cheltenham Spa. On Mondays, Fridays and Saturdays it turned left at Pleck Junction to stop at Walsall (11.45-11.50), where the engine change was made. It then followed a half-circle via Sutton Coldfield to join the Midland at Castle Bromwich and head south. This was to reduce congestion in New Street on the busier days of the week. Curiously enough this roundabout only took 6min longer than the Birmingham route, taking it past Camp Hill at 12.19. The slight time difference disappeared by the time it reached Cheltenham Spa Lansdown at 1.14 (MFS) or 1.13 (TWTh) and left at 1.19 after detaching the Southampton coach. It did not stop at Gloucester, going straight through to Bath (2.25-2.30). The run over the S&D was nominally nonstop to Broadstone (4.11-4.16), although a stop was made at Evercreech Junction to take water and detach the assisting engine if one was taken from Bath. Calling at Poole (4.22-4.26), it arrived

Above:
'Black Five' No 5440, the first on the S&D, here on a Sheffield-Bournemouth express south of Templecombe. A Midland clerestory coach has been pressed into use on this Saturday. *F. Moss*

at Bournemouth West at 4.36 (almost half an hour later than it had done 17 years before).

The northbound train left Bournemouth at 10.20 and made two-minute stops at Parkstone (10.26), Poole (10.32), Broadstone (10.42) and Blandford (11.1). Attaching the assisting engine at Evercreech Junction, it reached Bath at 12.30. In this direction it did stop at Gloucester (1.20-1.24), and at Cheltenham (1.35-1.40), to pick up the Southampton coach. There was also a stop at Bromsgrove, but not in the station, for this of course was to allow banking engines to buffer up behind and push it up the Lickey Incline. On Mondays to Fridays it ran up the Birmingham West Suburban line to enter New Street station, heading east, at 2.43, and out at 2.50 via Bescot to Crewe (3.56-4.6). Stopping to set down passengers at Stockport (4.36-4.40), it reached Manchester at 4.50. On Saturdays it took the Walsall route and arrival in Manchester was 15min later. The Liverpool portion did not get away from Crewe until 4.22, reaching Lime Street at 5.20. At least in this direction it was about as quick as in 1910.

The Southampton coach was conveyed on the back of the Great Western's 10.5am from Southampton Terminus, using running powers over the Southern Railway from Southampton to Andover Junction and the former Midland & South Western Junction Railway from there to Cheltenham, reached at 1.15pm. In order to make connection with the 'Pines' this train ran into Lansdown station instead of the GW terminus at St James'. It started back with the southbound coach at 1.35 and arrived at Southampton at 4.46. Although it made 10 stops and took 3hr 10min for the 96 miles, this train was booked as Class A, express passenger, the only one on that route.

We may take it that the results of these enhanced services were satisfactory, although the weather, critical to a seaside resort, did not help. The 1927 summer season started with a massive storm and a display of ball lightning over the sea front, and finished the same way, with two RAF Supermarine Southampton flying-boats wrecked while moored off the front. It was officially assessed as 'dismal'.

The elements notwithstanding, in the winter timetable, commencing on 26 September, the title 'Pines Express' appeared on a page headed 'FAMOUS LMS TRAINS' (note the publicity man's use of 'famous' for something he has just thought up). The chief differences from the summer service were that it included a southbound stop at Gloucester Eastgate, and went into Birmingham New Street every day. A connection was quoted for travelling from and to Walsall. A stop was also added at Blandford and arrival at Bournemouth was slightly later at 4.44, the northbound timing being unchanged.

Below:
The curve and three level crossings in Poole were awkward obstacles. 'Black Five' No 45440, still on the 'Pines' after 20 years, reaches Towngate Street while the train is still on the High Street crossing. Seen from the station platform. *O. J. Morris*

The 'Pines' arrived at New Street at the same time as the 8.15am Leeds-Bristol and then followed one block behind it down to Mangotsfield. The northbound train ran up that section a quarter of an hour ahead of the Paignton-Bradford 'Devonian'. There was an opportunity here to run a Bradford-Bournemouth through coach, switching it from one train to the other in New Street station, as they had the prewar York coach, and this was introduced on 7 May 1928. It ran only on Tuesdays, Wednesdays and Thursdays southbound and Wednesdays, Thursdays and Fridays northbound. On weekends the numbers of passengers from the north justified a complete train, and then the 'Pines' went via Walsall and could not make the connection.

The 'Pines', like its predecessor, never ran on Sundays.

There remained the anomaly that the southbound 'Pines' reversed in Birmingham while the northbound did not. (We have remarked on the flexibility of operation in the area, but if a train with coaches to be detached arrived unexpectedly in the wrong direction it would mess up the shunting arrangements and could

Above:
Shortly before electrification, a West Country train comprising Great Western coaches passes the deserted station at Heaton Norris on its way into Manchester. Heaton Norris Junction Box, just visible above the second coach, has a complete rig of LNWR lower quadrant signals. *N. F. Dyckhoff*

jam up the station.) This was thought undesirable, and in 1929 the route was changed. On Tuesday, Wednesday and Thursday it now forked right at Bushbury Junction to call at Wolverhampton High Level and use the Stour Valley line to enter New Street from the west. This enabled Wolverhampton folk to join it, but as the northbound still took the Bescot route they had to be content with a connecting train from Birmingham to take them back. On Mondays, Fridays and Saturdays (nb) and Saturdays (sb) it used the Walsall route. At this time the 'Pines' was said to form part of the Manchester-Birmingham services, of interest more to businessmen; when it went via Walsall an additional 10.5am Manchester-Birmingham was run to compensate for the loss.

In the winter the Wolverhampton (sb) and Bescot (nb) routes were used on all days. No, not all — the winter timetable began on 23 September but the northbound train ran via Walsall on Saturdays 28 September and 5 October, and the summer routeing began again on 1 June 1930, before the summer timetable commenced on 7 July. One wonders how, or if, the travelling public kept track of these variations; the railwaymen presumably did because they were told to.

Down in the south, the 'Pines' was the fastest train over the Somerset & Dorset, taking a few minutes over 2hr for the 71 miles, not quite making the 1hr 54min which had been attained before World War 1. The engines hauling it were still in the blue S&D livery which railway enthusiasts loved as a colourful exception to the uniformity imposed by the Grouping of the railway companies.

As a traffic source, the S&D was inconsiderable apart from the collieries in the Radstock area. The LMS recognised that its principal value was as a through route from the north and this alone justified its direct operating deficit of about £82,000 a year. From 1929 they tried to do something about that figure. They first tried to buy out the Southern's interest, on the grounds that since the latter did not run through trains it was of even less value to them. When that was declined they proposed to the Great Western a traffic pooling arrangement, covering places such as Bath, Shepton

Mallet, Wells or Highbridge where there was duplication of facilities, which would have made the GW virtually a partner in the S&D Joint Committee. The GW said, 'In effect, you want us to share your losses. No thanks.'

Then they looked for economies, and as from 1 January 1930 the Traffic Superintendent's office at Bath closed down, absorbed into the Bristol Division, and the engines owned by the Joint Committee were vested in the LMS. As a quid pro quo, the Southern took sole responsibility for the way and works. Another money-saving measure was the closure of Highbridge Works, so the blue livery came to an end.

During the 1930s the arrangement remained just about the same, so far as the passengers were concerned. There was a tendency to draw out the schedule times. This was the period when the country very gradually became more prosperous and the prospect of a holiday came within the reach of people who had never seen a green field in their lives. The railways became busier, train loads rose, and despite the provision of more powerful engines there was little choice but to reduce speeds. This was the period when Sir Harold Hartley and William Stanier wrought changes in the presentation of the train for the first time in over 30 years. From the end of 1934 steel-bodied coaches were hauled by larger, starkly functional, taper-boiler engines, the first of a type to become ubiquitously known as 'Black Fives'.

Not that the LMS managers were averse to attracting passengers. In 1928 they introduced a publication, *Holidays by LMS*, and did it properly. The usual lists of hotels and attractions, extensively illustrated, were complemented by maps by the foremost publisher in that field, John Bartholomew Ltd. It was not parochial but covered the whole country, over 600 pages, priced 6d. Ten years later it had grown to 976 pages but the price was unchanged. It now included a list of holiday schemes, precursors of the 'package holidays' of the next generation, in which the LMS made all the travel and accommodation arrangements. They had to be booked a minimum of 10 days in advance. There were 54 of them; No 5, Bournemouth, offered:

> 'Seven days Boarding House bed, breakfast, lunch and dinner, from dinner on Saturday to breakfast the following Saturday, plus three Coach Tours. Monday afternoon to Mudeford, Highcliffe Castle, Milford-on-Sea, Lymington, Brockenhurst, the New Forest, Beaulieu, Lyndhurst Road, Bank and Swan Green, Hinton St Michael and Christchurch. Wednesday all day, to Blandford, Sturminster Newton, Shepton Mallet, Wells Cathedral, Cheddar and the Caves, Glastonbury, Yeovil, Sherborne and the Blackmore Vale. Thursday afternoon to Lytchett Minster, Wareham, Lulworth Castle, Lulworth Cove and Wool.'

The price, per person, was £4 3s 6d, or £5 4s 6d if staying at a Private Hotel, with variable reductions for children and a supplement of 10s 6d for Easter Week and departures during August. That did not include rail travel. Monthly return tickets cost about 1d per mile, so the fare from Manchester was 42s return. Once there you could buy a Holiday Contract ticket, giving unlimited travel in the area for a week, for 10s.

Improvident potential holidaymakers were encouraged to 'Save to Travel by the LMS Investment Scheme' You could buy shilling stamps at any station or town office, sticking them in a folder provided; 10 stamps were exchanged for a voucher which bore interest at a rate of 5%, or 6d for its year's validity.

Also in this period the LMS ventured into the publicity book arena. The first title was, predictably enough, *The Royal Scot*, and the author was, equally predictably, S. P. B. Mais. It was on sale in mid-1928, so clearly Mr Loftus Allen had not been idle. There followed a 'route book', titled *On the Track of the Royal Scot* by Edmund Vale, sold in two parts. There were eventually five 'Tracks': Euston to Holyhead, Euston to Liverpool, Euston to Carlisle, Carlisle to Glasgow, St Pancras to Manchester. That was not as extensive as it looks, for the first three were largely the same in content — the concentration on London showing up again. They were very well written, with balanced coverage and lively anecdote, and it is a pity there were not more of them.

On summer Saturdays the 'Pines' was diverted to avoid Crewe station, by running on the lines normally used only by goods trains. They were known sometimes as the Tunnel Lines but more officially as the Independent Lines. Four tracks, designated Up and Down Slow, Up and Down Fast, diverged from the main line at Basford Hall Junction, 1½miles south of the station, and passed through the vast marshalling yard. Three signalboxes, Sorting Sidings South, Middle and North, controlled these lines. They crossed under the Shrewsbury main line to Salop Goods Junction, a secretive place in a cutting between the station and Crewe town centre. Here they split into three double

Above left:
The north end of Crewe station on 19 August 1955, with the Chester line going left in front of North Junction box, the Liverpool line going straight on and the Manchester line curving away right. *B. Morrison*

Left:
The northbound 'Pines' on Saturday 5 September 1959, nearing Castle Bromwich on its way round Birmingham. The engine is 'Black Five' No 44659. The first two coaches are a BR Standard BCK and a CK. Dimly seen on the extreme left is the main local landmark, Fort Dunlop. *M. Mensing*

Above:
The southbound 'Pines' at Perry Barr on 19 September 1956, making for New Street on the GJ line. The fifth coach is an LMS 12-wheeled diner. Engine No 46160 *Queen Victoria's Rifleman.* *M. Mensing*

Above right:
The flyover at Yate South Junction on 30 August 1952. The coaches on the bridge are early LMS wood-panelled stock, one still in LMS livery. They are in a Bristol-Birmingham train, possibly the 2.15pm, which has come up the GW route and is joining the Midland line. The southbound 'Pines', hauled by Bath's 'Black Five' No 44917, comes underneath. *G. Jefferson*

lines: the Liverpool Independent, which passed in two single-track tunnels under the area of Crewe North Junction to come up either side of the main line at Coal Yard Junction: the Manchester Independent, which passed through a double-track tunnel to emerge beside the Manchester main line and join it on a flat junction at Sydney Bridge — the route used by the 'Pines': and the Chester Independent, which rose steeply past the North Locomotive Depot to join the Chester main line not far from North Junction. All these lines were normally worked under Permissive Block Regulations, which meant basically that more than one train could be in a section at one time and could even draw up nose to tail. In order to pass the 'Pines' through, all the signalmen had to change over to Absolute Block

working, which was a great inconvenience. The instructions said that passenger trains were otherwise only to be sent this way in emergency.

In 1932 they devised a more radical method of avoiding Crewe when going north on summer Saturdays, diverting through Stoke-on-Trent. There was no intention to extend the service to the Potteries, for the train did not stop there. This important area was very badly served by the LMS; as late as 1941 the former North Staffordshire Railway main lines were still laid with 30ft-long rails, unable to carry the 'Royal Scot' and 4-6-2 type engines. While expresses raced over the unpopulated Cheshire plain, Stoke was left without through services to London or anywhere else at all distant. To see extra trains sailing by, disdaining them, must have been doubly irritating to waiting travellers at Stoke station.

This omission of the Crewe call on Saturdays was possible because there was no Liverpool portion to collect — it ran as a complete through train to and from Bournemouth. The preferred means of fitting it in was to use the 'Pines' weekday path. It made the Crewe stop,

and usually ran via Walsall. Northbound, it ran a quarter of an hour ahead of the 'Pines'.

In 1930 there was an instruction that the 'Pines' was not to carry passengers for Crewe from Manchester or Stockport, from which we may infer that they were now able to fill it with people travelling further. In the same vein, from 1929 if not earlier, stops at Stockport, Edge Hill and Mossley Hill were denoted pick-up only (sb) or set-down only (nb), to prevent the rude peasantry from using it as a local service.

In 1933 another variation was tried: using the Stour Valley line on Mondays and Saturdays but changing the engine at Wolverhampton and running through Birmingham without stopping. This would not have made much difference to the congestion problem at New Street and was not much used.

Although the Southern Railway controlled civil engineering on the S&D, this control did not extend to doing much about the configuration of Templecombe station, where it passed under the Southern main line. Providing a properly-appointed platform linked by steps or ramps to the main station immediately above was apparently too difficult. Throughout almost the whole life of the line the procedure was for northbound trains to pull up at Templecombe No 2 signalbox, where a pilot engine was attached to draw them back, round a corner into a platform in the upper station. Southbound trains ran direct into that platform and the pilot engine drew them out again before they continued their journey. It was done very expeditiously but it extended a two-minute stop into eight at the best. Passengers had not the least idea why this shuttling to and fro should be necessary and regarded it with either amusement or exasperation as an example of how railway companies naturally behaved. In 1937 the southbound 'Pines' began to make this call, the declared purpose being to provide a connection with the 12 noon Plymouth-Brighton express which called at 3.19pm.

By 1937, the last true summer of peace, they had all the 'Pines' permutations going at once, making it just about as complex as one train could be. Here goes:

Southbound

Tue/Wed/Thu. Start Manchester at 10am, pick up at Stockport. Start Liverpool at 9.40, pick up at Edge Hill, Mossley Hill and Runcorn. Combine at Crewe, via

5 July–26 September 1937			
Manchester LR	d 10am SX 9.55am SO	a 4.50 SX 5.36 SO	
Stockport	d 10.10 SX 10.5 SO	a 4.36 SX 5.22 SO	
Liverpool LS	d 9.40 SX	a 5.21 SX	
Crewe	d 10.45 SX	a 3.58 SX	
Wolverhampton HL	d 11.42 TWTh	-	
Birmingham NS	d 12.12pm TWTh	a 2.45 SX	
Cheltenham Spa	a 1.10	d 1.51 SX 2.1 SO	
Gloucester	a 1.22	d 1.37 SX 1.45 SO	
Bath	a 2.15	d 12.44pm	
Blandford	a 4.0	d 11.13	
Poole	a 4.24	d 10.47	
Parkstone	-	d 10.41	
Bournemouth W	a 4.37	d 10.35	
Ludgershall	a 3.45	d 11.24	
Andover Jn	a 4.1	d 11.9	
Southampton C	a 4.57	d 10.16	
Southampton T	a 5.5	d 10.10am	

Wolverhampton to Birmingham, drop off Manchester-Birmingham coaches and find another engine. Out of Brum via Camp Hill, stop at Cheltenham to drop the Liverpool-Southampton coach, and at Gloucester, to Bath and reverse. Over the S&D, putting off the pilot engine at Evercreech Junction, into Templecombe Upper

Left:
A view north from Lansdown Road,
Cheltenham. Lansdown station curves off to the
left; obscured by the signals is the bay used by
MSWJ trains. The train is the 12.26pm
Worcester-Gloucester of 20 July 1957, hauled
by Class 4 No 75058 of Leicester. *B. England*

Above:
On 20 May 1958 the northbound 'Pines' had
two of the highly-valued Standard 5s,
Nos 73050 (later preserved by the
Peterborough Railway Society) and 73051;
seen passing Henstridge. The use of stations
as junk-yards was well established even then.
R. J. Blenkinsop

and back out, to Blandford, Poole and Bournemouth,
arriving 4.37pm.
Mon/Fri. Same starting and finishing times, but from
Bushbury Junction to Walsall, thence via Castle
Bromwich to Camp Hill. This was allowed only 2min
more than the New Street route, absorbed from

Berkeley Road to Bath. No Manchester-Brum coaches,
SO the 10.5am runs.
Sat. Start Manchester at 9.55am, through the
Independent Lines at Crewe, to reach Walsall 9min
earlier than on Mon/Fri. Five minutes later by the time
we get to Bath, but into Bournemouth by 4.37pm. The
Liverpool train comes up to Crewe and goes forward at
10.49, in the 'Pines' Mon/Fri path, and follows the latter
all the way to Bournemouth.

Northbound.
Mon/Fri. Start Bournemouth at 10.35am, pick up at
Parkstone, Poole and Broadstone — rather a slow
process, 22min for the first eight miles — stop at
Blandford and Evercreech Junction (do not bother with
Templecombe), into Bath. On to Gloucester and
Cheltenham; the Southampton coach should have been
waiting for half an hour, giving it ample leeway for late
running. Enter Birmingham via Selly Oak and exit on the
Grand Junction via Bescot, which means we go through
New Street station in the same direction as the
southbound train on Tuesdays to Thursdays. Drop the
Liverpool coaches at Crewe, set down at Stockport and
arrive Manchester at 4.51pm. The Liverpool portion is

attached to the 8.45am Plymouth-Liverpool, which sets down at Runcorn, Mossley Hill and Edge Hill and gets in at 5.21pm.

Sat. 10.35am again from Bournemouth, but a quarter of an hour later as we climb the Lickey Incline. Through Camp Hill, round to Walsall for the engine change. Rejoin the main line to Bushbury Junction, turn right at Norton Bridge to Stone and on through Stoke. This brings us out on to the Manchester main line at Cheadle Hulme, to set down at Stockport and reach London Road at 5.36pm. The Liverpool train leaves Bournemouth at 10.20am and also runs via Walsall. However, it misses out Gloucester by crossing to the GW line at Standish Junction and passing the town on the avoiding line. Calls at Crewe, but not at Mossley Hill, reaching Liverpool at 5.35pm. On Saturdays 24 July to 4 September this train also conveys a Manchester portion.

16 June-5 October 1947			
	SX	SO	
Manchester LR	d 10.25am	d 10.25am	a 4.45 SX 5.0 SO
Birmingham NS	d 12.42		a 2.15 SX
Cheltenham Spa	a 1.37 d 1.42	a 1.56 d 2.2	a 1.9 d 1.15
Gloucester	a 1.51 d 1.56	a 2.11 d 2.18	a 12.52 d 12.58
Bath	a 2.45	a 3.10	d 12.3pm
Bournemouth W	a 5.5	a 5.30	d 9.45am
Birmingham			d 2.30pm SX
Derby			a 3.19 SX
Sheffield			a 4.23 SX

6 October 1947		
Manchester LR	d 10.20am	a 4.40
Liverpool	d 10.25	a 6.35 (not through carriages)
Birmingham NS	d 12.42pm	a 2.15
Cheltenham Spa	a 1.39 d 1.44	a 1.11 d 1.16
Gloucester	a 1.54 d 1.59	a 12.54 d 12.59
Bath	a 2.50	d 12.3pm
Bournemouth W	a 5.14	d 9.45am
Birmingham		d 2.35pm SO
Sheffield		a 4.36 SO
Derby		a 3.27 SO

Now imagine yourself as a roster clerk with the job of arranging guards' duties…

The Southampton-Cheltenham train was little changed from 10 years before, except that it was slightly quicker, a concept which to date was unique in the 'Pines' repertoire. It started at 10.10am and

Below:
A comparatively rare working of a 'Scot' on the 'Pines', No 46108 *Seaforth Highlander*, of Holyhead, on 19 September 1959. It is in Platform 4 on the LNW side of New Street, about to go towards Wolverhampton.
M. Mensing

Above:
In their early days the electric locomotives were given the sort of treatment we now give to preserved steam engines. On 27 September 1960, E3049 stands in Crewe station to take over the northbound 'Pines', with the train number already up, while AEI staff fuss round it, topping up the batteries with distilled water.
M. Mensing

made two more stops at Andover Town and Chiseldon. On the way back it reverted to character by taking 19min longer than in 1927.

In the late 1930s there were no Bradford coaches in the summer, as Bradford had a complete train. The hiving-off of the Liverpool portion was also done on the Thursday before Easter and the Friday before Whitsun. It was customary among observers to refer to it as the relief 'Pines' but that does not mean much, as any extra train on the route could be so described if one felt like it.

Incidentally, ours was not the only train to take different routes there and back. In summer 1939 the up 'Lancastrian' and down 'Mancunian', two of the Euston-Manchester expresses, were diverted via Stoke-on-Trent. But by then holiday time was running out and everyone knew it. The *Railway Magazine* was impressed by the cosmopolitan aspect of seeing the 1.35pm Cheltenham-Southampton comprising two GWR coaches, the LMS through coach and an SR coach carrying troops; but company pride was regarded as a dead letter and the British railways just called themselves British Railways.

In the autumn of 1937 Wolverton Works converted a train of coaches to an ARP Instruction Unit. On 16 January 1939 the Home Office ordered 400,000 domestic air raid shelters, most to be supplied by the railway workshops. There was no doubt as to what was coming, even though Lord Stamp told his staff it would

blow over. On 14 August LMS stations switched to reduced 'blackout' lighting. On 1 September the Government took control of the four railway Groups under the Emergency Powers (Defence) Act. It immediately announced wholesale reductions in passenger services, including most long-distance through trains. On the LMS the summer timetable continued until 10 September; on Monday 11th the 'Pines' and all through trains over the S&D ceased to run.

The reasons for this stoppage were various: to turn the British public's mind from frivolity to war, to release rail traffic capacity for war supply movements, and to free works repair capacity for munitions manufacture. During September alone some 260 LMS coaches were commandeered for civil and military ambulance train

use. The north-south routes were considered more or less reserved for military freight and troops, and even if anyone had the leisure for holidays, they would not spend them near what was now the front line, the south coast. Among the changes, the 'Black Fives' were withdrawn from the S&D, replaced by Southern Railway 'T9' 4-4-0s.

It is noticeable that the Southern, which was closest to the enemy, resisted the pressure to turn its facilities over to war work and kept up its services far more than the other companies. It received a lot of criticism for doing so, but as a result it recovered more quickly after

the war and played its part in rebuilding the nation while the rest of the railways were regarded as down-and-out wrecks. The demise of many lines such as the S&D really began not with Beeching, but in the 1940s.

After the initial cataclysm the authorities relented somewhat, and from 1 January 1940 through coaches resumed between Bournemouth and Bradford. The train used was the wartime equivalent of the 'Devonian', 9.30am Bradford-Bristol. The coaches were detached at Mangotsfield, taken down to Bath and put on the 4.25pm Bath-Bournemouth, arrival 7.30pm. Northbound they were on the 9.45am, reaching Bath at

Left:
Class 2 No 40652 assists No 34018 *Axminster*, rebuilt the previous autumn, on the northbound 'Pines' on 29 August 1959, passing Wellow with its notable church tower. At this point the line has a sawtooth profile which averages about level.
J. C. Beckett

a lot of retired army officers, were so upset at being ignored by the Luftwaffe that a British bomber dropped a stick of bombs across the town so that they should not feel so left out. What actually happened was that there was just one German attack and two buildings destroyed; a house by Alum Chine where Robert Louis Stevenson had lived, and the Lansdowne Hotel which was then a hostel for Canadian airmen. Poole, as a port, was of course heavily bombed.

With the European war drawing to a close, enhanced through services were put on from 7 May 1945. Two York-Bristol trains, 9.32pm and 10.20am, offered connections to Bournemouth, getting you there at 11.7am and 10.44pm respectively. By connecting services you could also go to and from Nottingham. The 9.30am Bradford-Bristol conveyed through coaches which were detached at Gloucester and taken forward by the 3.15pm to Bournemouth. On Saturdays there was a 9.52am from Leeds running right through to Bournemouth, using the same path over the S&D. One could join it at Birmingham by leaving Manchester at 10.20am. By taking the 1.40pm Bournemouth-Bristol one could use the 7.30pm Bristol-York and get a connection from Birmingham ending up in Manchester at 1.45am — a mere 12 hours' travelling. These long expeditions were not allayed by any creature comforts on board the train. During that summer the railway workshops began overhauling restaurant cars, but only a few were available to be put into service on 1 October.

For summer 1946, commencing on 6 May, the 'Pines' was back on Saturdays only, although it was not recognised by name. It was one of several through trains, the full list being as follows:

12.4pm, and on to Mangotsfield to be attached to the 12.35pm Bristol-Bradford.

In May 1941 the 9.45am was extended to Gloucester. From there one could take a Bristol-Sheffield train as far as Derby and a connection to Manchester Central at 8.46pm. There was a 3.15pm Gloucester-Bournemouth through train arriving at 7.37, which connected with a Derby-Bristol, which connected with the 8.55am from Manchester Central.

The Germans were not so daft as to think that Bournemouth was a vital part of the British war effort. There is a story that the inhabitants, doubtless including

Bournemouth arrivals	Bournemouth departures
1.10pm; 7.45am Birmingham	MSO 8.40am; Bradford 6.38pm
SO 2.50pm; 7.30am Nottingham	SO 9.45am; Manchester 5.4pm
SO 3.28pm; 10.5am Birmingham	SX 9.45am; Sheffield 4.42pm
SO 4pm; 9.20am Nottingham	SO 9.55am; Leeds 6.9pm
4.35pm; 9.20am Sheffield	SO 10.15am; Nottingham 6.15pm
SO 5.54pm; 9.45am Leeds	FSO 12.15pm; Nottingham 7.25pm
SO 7.15pm; 11am Manchester	
SO 6.35am; FO 8.30pm Bradford	

These provided a good service to the resort, bearing in mind that the country was still on a war footing, many men were still in the Forces and the railways were kept short of materials as a matter of Government policy. They also helped to liven up the S&D, adding to its four or five daily local trains. In the autumn they all ceased except the 'Pines', which was now attaining times comparable with its prewar schedule:

Manchester d 10am, Bournemouth a 5pm,
connection from Liverpool d 9.15am.
Bournemouth 9.45am, Manchester a 4.42pm,
through coach to Sheffield.

The only other through train was an 11.40am Bournemouth-Sheffield. There was nothing for Liverpool, and the Southampton coach was not revived.

The winter of 1946-7 was a terrible time in Britain. Shortages and rationing were worse than at any time during the war, thousands of men were being demobilised to find they had no jobs, no homes and no money, and those for whom tools and benches could be found were being continually exhorted to work harder — not for themselves but to pay for the war. In one of the coldest winters on record crops were frozen into the soil and coal stacks became solid mounds which had to be broken up by squads of men with picks and road-drills. Coal shortage forced the railways to curtail operations; naturally anything that smacked of leisure travel was the first to go. The 'Pines' was suspended from mid-January until Easter 1947.

. When it resumed it was more recognisably itself, although still without a title. Another route variation was used; southbound via Stoke, Bescot and Selly Oak, so it now headed west through New Street; northbound via Selly Oak, Bescot and Crewe on Mondays to Fridays, via Stoke on Saturdays. In contrast to the prewar arrangement, it always came into the Midland side at New Street. In both directions it ran via Walsall on Saturdays. However, it had lost the 10 o'clock departure

Left:
On Saturday 25 August 1962 the
northbound 'Pines', hauled by Class 5
No 73021, has crossed the River Rea at
Lifford and is heading for Camp Hill and
Walsall; two more runs to go on this
route. *P. J. Shoesmith*

time from Manchester, being now 10.25. On arrival in
Manchester it was scheduled to come into the Mayfield
excursion station. On Tuesdays to Fridays a northbound
portion, usually one coach, was conveyed for Sheffield.
It was detached at Birmingham and reached Sheffield at
4.36pm. There was no corresponding southbound
portion. (The presence of such one-way workings does
not mean that a pile of coaches grew at Sheffield in a
sort of railway sorcerer's apprentice performance; the
coaches found their way back in other services.)

From 6 October 1947 it was broadly the same but
simpler, going via Crewe and Bescot both ways on
every day, but the time away from Manchester was
changed yet again, to 10.20am. A good connection
from Liverpool was provided by means of the 10.25am
to Birmingham, which reached Crewe at 11.1 while the
'Pines' was waiting. In the return direction it was not
good, for on disembarking at Crewe at 3.34pm one had
to wait for either the 5.5 stopper or the 5.20 express to
Liverpool. The Sheffield-Bournemouth through coach
ran every day, conveyed in the 10.10am from Sheffield,
which arrived at New Street at 12.13. In a complete
inversion of the previous timetable, the coach to
Sheffield now ran on Saturdays only, in a train which left
New Street at 2.35pm and reached Sheffield at 4.36.

It was soon apparent that the formation of the British
Transport Commission Railway Executive did not
presage any change in outlook, for that body
immediately began describing anything that did not
start or finish in London as a 'cross-country' train. Those
on board, looking out at the endless miles of the Black
Country, now rendered even more desolate by the
amount of plant that had been bombed or worked to
destruction, were possibly not uplifted by the
knowledge that they were in the country. Nor was there
much success in welding the companies into one big,
happy family and one cannot help thinking that the
decline of all former 'joint' lines was not purely cold
commercial logic. The S&D was placed in the Southern
Region for engineering and traffic purposes, under the
Southampton District Office, but locomotives and
operating were under the London Midland Region with
an Assistant District Superintendent at Bath. In January
1950 the line from Bath to Cole became part of the
Western Region, operating was put under the Southern,
the locomotives 'on loan' from the London Midland.
From February the Southern was in charge of the
locomotive depots of Bath, Radstock, Templecombe,
Branksome and Highbridge, but their locomotives were
still under London Midland jurisdiction and remained so
until 1953. It is of course true that a heap of ash in the
bowels of an engine does not care what region it
belongs to, and with all the management reshuffles

going on it is unlikely that anyone up there gave much
thought to the man down below who had to shovel it
out on a wet winter night. Reorganisation did impinge
on the men when they were presented with Southern
'West Country' class locomotives to work their
expresses. Five years later, however, there was another
change-round when the WR/SR boundary was shifted to
just south of Templecombe, and Bath, Radstock,
Highbridge and Templecombe locomotive depots were
placed in the WR. That could have been a good thing,
as the WR had in its allocation a machine the SR knew
not, the Class 9F 2-10-0, which the men on the job
believed could save the S&D from closure. Anyone who
has spent any time in British industry will not need
telling what happens to the opinions of the men on
the job.

The Summer 1949 timetable commenced on 23 May
and at last the 'Pines Express' appeared in the literature
and on the sides of the coaches. It even got its
10 o'clock slot back. Shortage of serviceable rolling
stock was the reason given for continuing failure to
restore prewar levels of service, but they did manage
to introduce new trains to Bournemouth: from
Newcastle every day, and from Birmingham and Cardiff
on Saturdays. Liverpool was given a Saturday train to
Bournemouth, but no return working.

Poor old Liverpool — it had fallen far from its heady
days at the turn of the century when it was the world's
foremost port, had not diversified like Manchester and
was viewed from elsewhere as just a problem,
mouldering on the coast between Southport and Rhyl.
But after a lapse of over 10 years, its through coaches
were restored to the 'Pines' on 5 June 1950. Departure
was at 10.15am, the return left Crewe at 3.48pm. As
before, on Saturdays an independent train went right
through, 10.30am from Liverpool and 10.25am from
Bournemouth, the latter including a through portion
for Manchester.

A couple of years later the Sheffield portion was
improved to run every day in both directions, but
working it right through from Bradford was another
prewar feature which was not restored.

During 1949-50 British Railways pursued a general
policy of stopping long-distance trains at stations on the
rims of the great conurbations, to attract the growing
numbers of dwellers in suburbia. The 'Pines' was one of
those so treated, the stations being Wilmslow and
Mossley Hill.

It was important enough to survive the vicissitudes
of the next few years, which by no means all services
did. Coal shortage remained a chronic problem; from
12 February 1951 many trains were cancelled and on-
train catering ceased. The 'Pines' was one of those cut,
to be restored on 19 March. (That day the
Bournemouth-Bath-Bournemouth section was worked
for the first time by a 'West Country' class engine.) By
the autumn of 1951 passenger train mileage was being
cut in order to give priority to the movement of freight.
For the same reason the 1951 summer season was put
back at short notice from 18 June to 2 July, and the
1952 season curtailed to 30 June to 14 September. This

was a matter of great concern to holiday resorts. British Railways did not seem to be making any progress.

Things to come were, however, taking shape in the bleak Pennine uplands. In 1954 Manchester London Road saw a new sight, overhead wires, and heard a new sound, the hum of electric locomotives, working through Woodhead New Tunnel to Penistone; the first electrification on the 1,500V dc overhead system recommended by the Weir Committee. On 11 June 1956 a new service began, a 12.10pm from Sheffield Victoria to Bournemouth. The thing to note about this is that it came up the Great Central line to Woodford Halse, over to Banbury and on through Oxford and Basingstoke. That may not have attracted the attention of men in Gloucester or Bath; only when seen in hindsight does it become significant.

One thing about British Railways, it did seem to be a bit more honest with the public (who, it was said, were now its owners). For instance, it now admitted that the 'Pines' stopped at Evercreech Junction. Another postwar feature was a northbound stop at Stalbridge; not because that village had sprung into prominence as a resort, but because it there overtook, and was advertised as connecting with, the 8.50am Bournemouth-Templecombe.

1957, the summer that saw passenger figures rise to an all-time high on British Railways, saw the 'Pines' starting from Manchester and Liverpool simultaneously at 10.15am. The reason was the inclusion from Stockport to Crewe of 10min Recovery Time, a device

which in essence allowed the driver and signalmen to bring the train into Crewe at any time between 10.58 and 11.8; if the latter, achieving a breakneck start-to-stop average speed of 37½mph. Proceeding via Bescot and Selly Oak, Bournemouth did not come into sight until half-past five. On Saturdays it ran via Stoke (no stop, of course) and Walsall, and a separate 10.30am from Liverpool followed it. The latter had a Manchester portion, starting at 10.28am, and on the peak Saturdays from 6 July to 10 August that also ran as a separate train. The northbound route was the same. Liverpool coaches were transferred to the 8am from Plymouth, which stopped at Hartford (possibly for no better reason than that this station happened to have its platforms on the Fast lines) and Runcorn. The Manchester portion made the Wilmslow stop, illogically since it did not do so southbound, and ran into Mayfield. On Saturdays it ran as usual via Walsall and Stoke, with a separate 9.25am Bournemouth-Liverpool & Manchester.

Sheffield and York had their own Saturday services. However, on Tuesdays to Thursdays, and on every day during the winter timetable, Sheffield coaches still ran in the 'Pines' in both directions, serving also Chesterfield, Derby and Burton upon Trent, and picking up (but not setting down) at Tamworth. The Sheffield-Birmingham train started at 10.10am, and the return train arrived at 4.36pm, the same timings as in previous years. On Mondays and Fridays it was extended through to and from Bournemouth, running a quarter of an hour ahead of the 'Pines' both ways.

There was no longer any pretence that any 'Pines' variants were part of the Manchester-Birmingham services; in fact their arrival at New Street was not even advertised and the northbounds were specified to set down only. Manchester-Birmingham coaches were not run, the only provision for travellers on the northern section being, on weekdays, some Manchester-Crewe coaches which were removed before the Liverpool portion was attached, or put on after the latter was detached. The 10.15am from Liverpool ran through to Birmingham, following the 'Pines' up from Crewe.

Although the speeds required were no greater than prewar, there was perhaps a feeling that they might be, for the 'Pines' was now prohibited from conveying any four-wheeled vehicles north of Bath. Mind you, there is no pictorial evidence that it had ever done so.

Fares in 1957 were, for long journeys, slightly less than 1¾d per mile second class, the Manchester-Bournemouth return fare being £3 5s 6d second, £4 18s 3d first. There was a variety of Cheap Day Tickets, Excursion Tickets, Walking-Tour Tickets and Circular Tour Tickets at lower rates. Luggage despatched at the departure station for delivery to your destination cost 2s 6d per item, or 5s for collection from home and delivery. There was a range of seven-day Holiday Runabout Tickets for areas about 30 miles across, for 17s 6d.

Came the year 1958, the builders moved in on the North Western side at London Road. This was the new start everyone had been waiting for, from clerks shivering in dingy, century-old offices to drivers poking oil feeders into greasy machinery by the light of flare lamps, not to mention travellers queuing at ticket windows in sulphur-laden smogs. Electrification! The spirit of the age was proclaimed in the Commission's propaganda film *The Third Sam*: Sam the engine driver emerged from the dark past to take his place in the sun and go sailing along with a smile on his face and nary a stain on his new uniform. The reality was that the Railway Executive had to say, 'Well, travel will soon be revolutionised but just at the moment you will have to put up with slower services, diversions and weekend closures, because we have to rebuild the railway while still using it.' 'Pines' users would be unimpressed; their service had been getting slower since 1917.

The loop line from Slade Lane Junction to Wilmslow via Styal was used as a proving-ground for the new system, which used overhead wires at 25,000V ac. It was energised in mid-1959. Conversion of the main

Left:
The Bournemouth Railway Club suggested putting *Evening Star* on the last S&D 'Pines', and on the day they were out on the lineside. There was quite a crowd at Midford to see her come through the tiny station and onto the double track, the driver opening her full out to attack the 1 in 60. Note the incorrect headlamps. The immaculate state of the way and works is a tribute to the pride felt by S&D men in their railway. *R. Puntis*

Above:
The last northbound 'Pines' in Walsall, Saturday 8 September 1962. Class 5 No 44659 worked from Bath to Walsall and is seen here on the curve from Lichfield Road Junction to Ryecroft Junction.
J. Haddock

Manchester-Crewe line was a costly job; two tunnels in Stockport were opened out into cuttings because they did not have enough height for the overhead wires. As part of the new image, London Road station was extensively overhauled, during which most of its trains were diverted to Victoria and Central or, as was done with the 'Pines', into the Mayfield excursion platforms. On 12 September 1960 it was reopened under the name of Manchester Piccadilly (Piccadilly is a square off the north end of London Road, further from the station). The Manchester, South Junction & Altrincham station was incorporated in it, and Mayfield was relegated to a parcels depot.

The speed limit was raised from 75 to 90mph and running time was cut by about 10min: quite spectacular for a trip of only 30 miles, although the 'Pines' schedule was still slightly slower than it had been in 1927. By the summer of 1961 all trains between Crewe and

Manchester, except those not stopping at Crewe, were electrically hauled, and the engineers moved on to the next phase: Crewe to Liverpool Lime Street. Electric working on this line began on 18 June 1962.

For those who were young in the years around 1957 to 1960, it was a time when travel, especially holiday travel, was at its best, whether by train or car. Shortages and rationing were at last forgotten, unemployment was at an all-time low, and the population was not high enough to exert intolerable pressure on the countryside. You could drive through Dorset, or Gloucestershire or Cheshire, for miles without meeting another vehicle, while for those who could not use a car the railway network still gave reasonable access to most areas. Birmingham was still black with coal smoke and ringing with the noise of metal-bashing in sweat-shops, but there was plenty of room on Bournemouth beach.

In the autumn and winter of 1960 the rough weather disrupted railway work everywhere. On the S&D the track slid down the hillside near Midford and the line was closed altogether from 5 to 9 December. The 'Pines' was sent on a tortuous route through Wimborne, Fordingbridge, Salisbury, Westbury, Bath GW, Bristol East, Lawrence Hill, and Westerleigh Junctions to regain its normal route at Yate. Inexplicably, the engines were booked to work right through from Birmingham to Bournemouth, which was not a good idea, as on the second day a 'West Country' ran out of coal soon after leaving Salisbury on the journey south. After that the engines were changed at Gloucester. 'Hall' class No 4942 *Maindy Hall* worked the northbound turn on the 6th and south on the 7th, the only known occasion when a Great Western engine hauled the 'Pines' before 1962.

From 12 September 1960, 'Pines' passengers could enjoy riding behind electric, diesel and steam locomotives in one journey. They probably did not appreciate it, for steam power in particular was now seen by the public as representative of all that was wrong with the railways. Images of clouds of steam over the Mendips and grimy firemen shovelling coal into engines puffing slowly up hills were strictly for bedtime stories; in real life they wanted speed. All eyes were on the possibilities for north-south travel by car opened up by the new London-Birmingham motorway, and the travelling public were not much concerned one way or the other by the announcement that caused such anguish in the small railway community of Somerset and Dorset. From 10 September 1962 the 'Pines Express' was to take a completely new route south of Crewe: to Nantwich and on to the former Great Western line through Market Drayton, Wellington, Wolverhampton Low Level, Birmingham Snow Hill, Oxford, Reading West curve, Basingstoke and Southampton to Bournemouth. Completely new? What nobody said was that in fact it was a reversion to the route of the original GW train of 1910.

16 September 1957-8 June 1958

Manchester LR	d 10.15am	a 4.45
Stockport	d 10.27	a 4.32
Wilmslow		a 4.18
Liverpool	d 10.15	a 4.50
Runcorn		a 4.28
Hartford		a 4.10
Crewe	d 11.13	a 3.41
Sheffield	d 10.10	a 5.2 SX 4.41 SO
Chesterfield d 10.31	a 4.39 SX 4.17 SO	
Derby	d 11.9	a 4.0 SX 3.38 SO
Burton	d 11.26	a 3.42 SX 3.21 FSO
Tamworth	d 11.44	
Birmingham NS	d 12.40pm	a 2.25
Cheltenham Spa	a 1.39	d 1.16
Gloucester	a 1.58	d 12.57
Bath	a 3.0	d 12.1pm
Shepton Mallet		d 11.18
Evercreech Jn	a 4.2	d 11.2
Stalbridge		d 10.38
Blandford Forum	a 4.53	d 10.20
Broadstone	a 5.12	
Poole	a 5.20	d 9.54
Bournemouth W	a 5.32	d 9.45am

117 June-15 September 1957

	SX	SO	SX	SO
Manchester LR	d 10.15am	d 10.20am	a 4.45	a 5.40
Stockport	d 10.27	d 10.33	a 4.32	a 5.24
Wilmslow			a 4.17	
Liverpool LS	d 10.15		a 4.50	
Runcorn			a 4.28	
Hartford			a 4.10	
Crewe	d 11.12		a 3.41	
Birmingham NS	d 12.40pm		a 2.25	
Cheltenham Spa	a 1.39	a 2.7	d 1.16	
Gloucester	a 1.58	a 2.23	d 12.57	d 1.15
Bath	a 3.0	a 3.25	d 12.1pm	d 12.5pm
Shepton Mallet			d 11.18	
Evercreech Jn	a 4.2	a 4.26	d 11.2	d 11.4
Stalbridge			d 10.38	
Blandford Forum	a 4.53	a 5.20	d 10.20	d 10.20
Broadstone	a 5.12	a 5.43		
Poole	a 5.20	a 5.53	d 9.54	d 9.54
Bournemouth W	a 5.32	a 6.8	d 9.45am	d 9.45am

3

'Pines' in Retreat, 1962-1967

Portrait of the Pines Express

Bournemouth in 1962 was little changed as a resort from the pre-war town but there was a subtle shift of emphasis. The 'new' industries based on electronics, cars and aircraft were moving in, houses and trading estates were spreading, traffic congestion and road improvements were priority topics. You would not have expected the old Bournemouth of boarding houses and retirement homes to be reading advertisements for factory sites — nor cinema posters for 'Pamela Green in her first nudist picture *Naked as Nature Intended* (Eastmancolor)' — but at the same time traditional interests still mattered. The demise of the S&D was viewed as the loss of an access facility for visitors, and aroused a good deal of indignation.

The decision to reroute the 'Pines' was part of a very large plan, which had four major objectives:

(1) to facilitate the full change to diesel haulage;

(2) to shift traffic off the LNW routes through Birmingham and the Euston-Crewe main line, to reduce interference with and from electrification work;

(3) to concentrate services from the north, those to South Wales and the West Country on the Birmingham & Gloucester, and those to the South Coast on the Oxford-Basingstoke route;

(4) to improve services on the Basingstoke-Southampton line, which was ripe for development. The population of Hampshire increased by 12% from 1951 to 1961, twice the national average.

The first objective may seem to be a *non sequitur* in relation to the S&D; would not diesel power provide

Below:
The first southbound 'Pines' on the new route on Monday 10 September 1962. It had 13 coaches and was taken from Wolverhampton to Oxford by No 5033 *Broughton Castle*; seen here at Acocks Green. *M. Mensing*

the answer to the working expense problem posed by that line and save it from closure? It might, were it not for Newton's Third Law. Yes, if you double the installed power on the train, you give it the potential for a much higher absolute performance — but double the power means double the force, and Mr Newton pointed out that at the point of application (the wheel on the rail) the force propelling the train is experienced equally and conversely by the track. Do that occasionally on a line like the S&D and you increase wear a little; do it regularly and rails creep, ballast breaks up, mud works up into ballast in cuttings, sleepers pump and ride quality goes; do it every hour and the whole railway will start sliding down the hillsides. To accept the enormous increase in power of diesel locomotives, the railway must be made correspondingly stronger; and even if you rebuild it from the ground up, the curves and single-line sections remain to restrict speed and load capacity. The GWR and LMS did look in some detail, in 1943 and 1947, at a plan to make a new northern end for the S&D. It included a new station on the site of the GW goods yard, a 1¾-mile tunnel from there under Widcombe and Claverton Down to Limpley Stoke and a reconstruction of the branch through Monkton Combe to join the S&D at Midford, thus bypassing Combe Down and Devonshire Tunnels. BR considered it again in 1958 but it would have entailed great expense and land acquisition in a built-up area, and they could never have spent that kind of money to benefit Radstock when Southampton was waiting for electrification. So the S&D remained a steam line and the expresses left it.

For the South Coast, the change was if anything one for the better. Southampton once more had a through train from Liverpool and Manchester. It even offered a connection to the Isle of Wight, via a Brockenhurst stop, Lymington and the ferry to Yarmouth. Ironically, it was now far more of a 'Pines Express' than before, for whereas the approach from Blandford was through ordinary English farmland, the new 'Pines' entered the New Forest at Totton and ran through rolling pine-clad country for some 20 miles.

All that notwithstanding, Bournemouth was not amused. The *Daily Echo*, now called the *Evening Echo*, printed on 1 September a letter from W. J. Andrew, who declared that the people 'completely fail to see how Bournemouth is to prosper by renaming a train, travelling on a completely different route, "The Pines Express" when that route is already served by the same train without a name. [He may have been thinking of the 9.30am to Birkenhead.] This is certainly not going to help...people to come to Bournemouth for their holidays...would like to know how the numerous extra summer service trains from Birmingham, Crewe, etc, are to be accommodated over an already overcrowded line, unless by that time Dr Beeching has frightened enough passengers from

the railways so as to make the running of these trains unnecessary!'

In his last supposition he was quite right. Dr Beeching himself was on record as stating that he preferred to see a train carrying 100 passengers each paying £5 than 500 passengers each paying £1, and summer holiday travellers were business that BR did not want.

Enthusiasts said that without the 'Pines' the S&D service was inadequate for the needs of the district, but this was specious; for many years the through

18 June-9 September 1962				
	SX	SO	SX	SO
Manchester P	d 10.30am	d 10.35am	a 4.38	a 5.40
Stockport	10.41	10.38	4.25sd	5.25sd
Liverpool LS	d 10.15		a 4.41	
Runcorn			4.20	
Hartford			4.9	
Crewe	11.19		3.43	
Birmingham NS	12.45pm		2.18	
Cheltenham Spa	1.43		1.15	
Gloucester	2.3	2.23	12.57	1.10
Bath	3.3	3.25	12.1pm	12.5pm
Evercreech Jn	4.5	4.26	11.6	11.4
Stalbridge		4.55		
Blandford Forum	4.53	5.20	10.19	10.19
Broadstone	5.12	5.43		
Poole	5.20	5.55	9.54	9.54
Bournemouth W	a 5.32	a 6.8	d 9.45am	d 9.45am

10 September 1962-16 June 1963		
Manchester P	d 10.0am	a 5.11
Stockport	a 10.8: d 10.11	a 4.54
Wilmslow		4.46
Liverpool LS	d 9.40	a 5.17
Runcorn	10.2	4.55
Hartford		4.41
Crewe	a 10.40: d 10.50	a 4.14: d 4.24
Wolverhampton LL	12.5pm	3.0
Birmingham SH	12.29	2.34
Leamington Spa	1.0	1.56
Banbury		1.25
Oxford	2.4	12.48
Reading West	d 2.46	a 12.6pm
Basingstoke	a 3.12: d 3.14	a 11.34: d 11.37
Winchester	3.41	11.6
Southampton	a 4.2: d 4.6	a 10.41: d 10.43
Brockenhurst	a 4.27: d 4.29	a 10.20: d 10.21
New Milton	4.41	10.10
Christchurch	4.51	9.58
Pokesdown	4.58	9.53
Boscombe	5.2	9.49
Bournemouth C	a 5.6: d 5.8	a 9.43: d 9.45
Bournemouth W	a 5.18	d 9.35am
Crewe	d 10.53am	
Stafford	d 11.26	
Wolverhampton HL	a 11.56: d 12.0	
Dudley Port	a 12.9: d 12.15pm	
Birmingham NS	a 12.34	

Above:
A rare view of the 'Pines' on the Market Drayton route; northbound at Tern Hill on 27 October 1962. This view contains a wealth of detail of a typical country station — goods office, cattle pen, two varieties of goods lock-up, GWR signal, notices, etc. This station kept the line going for a while by virtue of the adjoining airfield. *IAL*

trains had not borne any connection with local traffic and what was really feared was that without them the small number of local users could not sustain the railway. That eventually proved to be the case.

On Friday 7 September the *Echo* announced, '"Pines" last trip over old S&D line. Tomorrow the "Pines Express" will leave Bournemouth West at 9.45am for Manchester, travelling for the last time via its time-honoured route.'

On Saturday the Class 9F 2-10-0 No 92220 *Evening Star*, driven by Peter Smith and fired by Aubrey Punter, pulled away from the West on one of the most publicised runs of a regular train ever. No pilot was taken over the Mendips, and the load of 426 tons was a record for one engine. Timekeeping was unfortunately marred by a 10min stop caused by the preceding 9.25am to Liverpool, also '9F'-hauled, which did badly and had to take an unscheduled pilot. From Bath, 'Black Five' No 44659 took over for the run to Walsall. After refuelling at Bath, Driver Peter Guy and Fireman Ron Hyde took *Evening Star* back on the southbound 'Pines' and roared out of Bath to the cheers of the crowd and a fusillade of exploding detonators. By Combe Down the fire was so hot that the doors jammed and had to be opened with the coal-pick. At Evercreech Junction Mr Andrew (of the above letter) placed a wreath on the engine, and as

the steam dispersed and the hum of the wheels faded, all that was left was folklore.

The front page of the *Echo* was dominated by the event, with a picture of Father Pedrick of Blandford and his dog (the dining car chefs used to hand him out the bones left from dinner) both wearing black ties. On the following Monday Driver Guy and Fireman Hyde were again on the front page, on the 'Pines', taking it out of Central station for the first time with engine No 34043 *Combe Martin*. A new Bournemouth-York service was started the same day.

By contrast, the changes at the north end attracted little comment. To the British Public, replacing the tedious trundle round by Sutton Coldfield with one equally tedious through Wellington made no difference. The simulacrum of a Manchester-Birmingham express was maintained by detaching a

39

Above left:
The southbound 'Pines' passing Tilehurst in the Thames Valley on 27 July 1963, hauled by a 'Merchant Navy'. The crew of No 35002 *Union Castle* have omitted to remove the train number MO4 tied on their smokebox door for the northbound run. *R. C. Riley*

Left:
The northbound 'Pines' coasting through Brockenhurst in the autumn of 1965. 'Merchant Navy' No 35011 *General Steam Navigation* was a regular performer on this job until scrapped in February 1966. *J. D. Gomersall*

Above:
One of the New Forest ponies with a youngster (and another on the way by the look of her). Another holiday train from the north, the 9.5am Birkenhead-Poole, ascends the 1 in 103 bank from Lymington Junction. 'Castleman's Corkscrew' diverges left in the distance; the line visible beyond the front steps of No 34053 *Sir Keith Park* (later preserved and now on the West Somerset Railway) is the Lymington branch. *V. L. Murphy*

portion from the southbound train at Crewe and sending it up the old route to Stafford and Wolverhampton High Level to terminate in Birmingham New Street, running up the Stour Valley line at the same time as the main train was in parallel with it on the GW line. At Oxford, which was complaining with rising stridency that it was badly served, it would appear as an improvement.

What irritated the public, though, was the journey time. The new route was 11 miles longer from Manchester to Birmingham and took an extra quarter of an hour; average speed 39mph southbound, 38mph northbound. Birmingham to Bournemouth was six miles further and took seven minutes less southbound but 19min more northbound. The pathing problem would account for the anomaly. Overall, you had a 4min longer trip south and 33min longer north, although a consolation was that the Saturday schedule was now the same as the weekday, so then you were a good half-hour better off. The whole performance was substantially slower than in the gloomy days just after the war. And this on a railway that claimed to be investing millions of money and revolutionising travel!

The Western Region was quite proud of its new acquisition and identified it by name in its Working

Timetable (the Great Western was the only grouped company to show train names in the WTT and the WR was the same). Smartly turned-out 'Castle' class engines with headboards were a marked contrast to the LMR engines from which they took over at Wolverhampton. It was the intention to use diesels, but the 'Western' class diesels were not ready and for the next couple of years the usual motive power was electric to Crewe, a 'Peak' class diesel or LMR 4-6-0 to Wolverhampton, a WR 4-6-0 to Oxford and a 'West Country' to Bournemouth. Some of the latter were in the form in which they had been rebuilt from 1957 onwards, which now appeared on the 'Pines' for the first time, as they had been 'unrebuilt' in the old S&D days. At first the Southern men were persuaded to put up the headboard on their engine but that did not last long, and headboards disappeared altogether when the steam engines went.

The new version comprised Manchester and Liverpool portions, with no coaches to or from the northeast. It made stops at Birmingham Snow Hill — without any shunting — Leamington Spa, Reading West, Basingstoke, Winchester and Southampton. West of Brockenhurst, it halted very briefly at New Milton, Christchurch, Pokesdown and Boscombe, becoming in effect a stopping train. It took 37min down and 35min up to cover those 15 miles, which wiped out the impression created by fast running on the rest of the new route. Travellers were not making use of these intermediate calls, so for the summer 1963 timetable, beginning on 17 June, they and the Brockenhurst stop were eliminated. The train now ran nonstop between Southampton and Bournemouth,

Below:
In 1964 a new bridge was built across the River Test at Redbridge. No 6978 *Helperley Hall* crosses with the Newcastle-Bournemouth on 16 July. The old bridge is being removed, and 0-6-0T No 30071, renumbered DS238 for Engineers' use, stands on it with wagons. *M. J. Fox*

Above right:
The 13.11 Portsmouth-Wolverhampton on 14 August 1965, comprising BR and Southern Railway coaches hauled by 'Black Five' No 45263. It followed the same route as the 'Pines' and is seen under the A33 road bridge after leaving Basingstoke. *G. D. King*

Below right:
On Wednesday 1 March 1967 the northbound 'Pines' calls at Birmingham Snow Hill. Brush Type 4 No D1701, from Old Oak Common, has a small 'W' painted below the number, to show staff in the London Midland Region that if it breaks down it is not their problem. *IAL*

taking 36min down and 32min up. The northbound also stopped at Banbury and Wilmslow but the southbound did not. The Liverpool portion called at Runcorn and, northbound only, Hartford. A separate Liverpool train still ran on summer Saturdays.

More changes were on the way. The passage of a stream of heavy trains through Market Drayton was certainly not a portent of times to come, while the passengers would not have been reassured if they had realised that they were riding on tracks already being run down towards abandonment. The route from Nantwich to Wellington was closed to passenger traffic as from 9 September 1963. The 'Pines' was now sent an even longer way round, out to Shrewsbury and back again, an extra 10½ miles. This was not done to benefit Shrewsbury; on Saturdays its presence in that town was not even admitted to the public and it stopped only to change the crew. For this function it pulled up on the through roads in the station: the down road in the middle between the main platforms and the up road on the east side behind the wall which once supported an overall roof.

At the same time there was a drastic speed-up on the Birmingham-Oxford leg. Fifteen minutes were cut from the schedule, a lot for 66 miles, raising the

average speed from 45½ mph to 55mph, an advertisement for diesel traction. Aware that people are more impatient to reach their holiday resort than they are to get home, the authorities did not gild this lily; they left the northbound schedule as it was.

A new routeing was brought in for summer Saturdays — not totally new but a revival of an old one. Coming up from Manchester the train took to the Crewe Independent Lines at Sydney Bridge Junction, went underneath and stopped on the curve between Salop Goods Junction and Gresty Lane No 1. Here the electric locomotive was exchanged for a diesel.

Top management had really got the taste for reorganising now and the next change was to transfer the Western Region lines north of Aynho into the London Midland Region. This had little effect on the men on the job, although it probably accelerated the replacement of 'Western' class locomotives by new Brush Type 4s. Administratively, it meant that the Western Region was no longer involved in the north-south through services, apart from the practical matter of passing them through its territory. The reorganisations were of course a result of the immense pressure on BR to cut costs. The response of any industry to that is to appoint numbers of well-paid managers, whose task is to find shop-floor jobs that can be eliminated, and BR was no exception. One of the decisions was to concentrate investment where it would do most good, which meant produce most income.

Bournemouth West station did not so much shut down as fade away. Trains stopped using it after 4 September 1965 without any formal procedure; it was abandoned on 4 October and was finally declared closed on 1 November 1965 to make way for a road, part of a town centre bypass, which cut across just south of the carriage sidings. The station site was taken for a car park. In common with most of its trains, the 'Pines' was extended to terminate at Poole, stopping also at Branksome and Parkstone. The empty stock ran back from Poole into the depot. This was a logical move; Poole was a boom town, expanding as fast as it could chew up the surrounding woods and fields, and should not have trains turning back outside

its boundary.

Fares were now at about 3¼d per mile second class, making the Manchester-Bournemouth return fare £7 4s second and £10 16s first. There was also a Mid-week Period Return, at £5 16s for adults and £1 16s for children.

By late 1965 things were heading for another alteration. The Western had achieved complete dieselisation and was getting very irritated by steam engines coming in from both north and south. Train names were seen as an anachronism, meaning nothing to the public and contributing nothing to revenue, to be phased out as quickly as could be done without attracting the attention of the Press and provoking 'good old days' feature articles. The words 'The Pines Express' were relegated to small print alongside the times in the LMR timetable, and to footnotes in the Inter-regional pages.

Two modernisation projects were in full swing: the huge London-Birmingham-Crewe and the Woking-Bournemouth electrifications. To exploit these to the full it would obviously be preferable to make passengers from the Midlands travel up to Euston, across London to Waterloo and down to Bournemouth.

The 'Pines' was allocated a diesel locomotive for its Southern leg from April 1966 but in practice it was often steam-hauled, a Standard Class 5 being seen on the job as late as 18 February 1967. Its long-time companion, the York-Poole, was still a steam turn and, owing to a growing shortage of Southern steam engines, was hauled alternately by a Southern 'West Country' and an LMS 'Black Five' between Banbury and Bournemouth. As a consequence, the latter class was occasionally seen at Waterloo. Because there was no

18 April 1966-5 March 1967

	SX	SO	SX	SO
Manchester P	d 10.0	d 10.0	a 17.06	a 17.19
Stockport	d 10.11	d 10.10	a 16.53	a 17.05
Wilmslow	d 10.17		a 16.44	a 16.55
Liverpool LS	d 09.45		a 17.11	
Runcorn	d 10.3		a 16.51	
Hartford			a 16.40	
Crewe	d 10.54	d 10.54	a 16.08	d 16.14
Shrewsbury	d 11.35		a 15.26	
Wellington	a 11.49: d 11.50	a 11.46: d 11.50	a 15.12: d 15.14	a 15.12
Wolverhampton LL	a 12.17: d 12.20	a 12.17: d 12.20	a 14.46: d 14.50	a 14.46: d 14.50
Birmingham SH	a 12.40: d 12.43	a 12.40: d 12.43	a 14.23: d 14.28	a 14.23: d 14.28
Leamington Spa	a 13.05: d 13.08	a 13.05: d 13.08	a 13.48: d 13.51	a 13.46: d 13.51
Banbury			a 13.25: d 13.28	a 13.25: d 13.28
Oxford	a 13.56: d 14.04	a 13.56: d 14.04	a 12.47	a12.47
Reading West	d 14.45	d 14.45	a 12.03: d12.06	d 12.03: d 12.06
Basingstoke	a 15.08: d 15.09	a 15.08: d 15.09	a 11.39: d11.41	a 11.39: d 11.41
Winchester	15.35	15.35	d 11.08	d 11.09
Southampton C	a 15.54: d 15.58	a 15.54: d 15.59	a 10.39: d 10.43	a 10.43: d 10.45
Bournemouth C	a 16.44: d 16.51	a 16.47: d 16.51	a 09.57: d 10.02	a 10.01: d 10.06
Branksome	a 17.01	a 17.00	d 09.49	d 09.53
Parkstone	a 17.05	a 17.06	d 09.43	d 09.48
Poole	a 17.10	a 17.10	d 09.38	d 09.42

Above right:
On the last day but one, Friday 3 March 1967, the southbound 'Pines' just after passing Tyseley station. The locomotive is Brush Type 4 No D1700. The first coach is an LMS postwar brake third, with the characteristic round lavatory window.
M. Mensing

Below right:
The rear of the same train, with the seventh coach, the kitchen/first diner, on the right. Tyseley station and signalbox are in the background.
M. Mensing

Sunday 'Pines' or York, the engines which came to Bournemouth on Saturday were spare on Sunday, and the Southern would use them for London turns, including the 'Bournemouth Belle'. On 27 June 1966 'Black Five' No 45349 worked from Bournemouth to Waterloo and back in place of the expected Brush diesel. The York-Poole was rerouted from Sheffield via Birmingham New Street and Worcester to Oxford on 5 September 1966, and ceased steam haulage.

The last 'Pines' steam working at its northern end took place on 14 February 1967. Brush diesel D1844 broke down at an unrecorded location on the way north, and Class 8F 2-8-0 No 48205 hauled it and the 12-coach train into Crewe, working the 570-ton load up to the line speed limit of 60mph.

The overhead electric wires in the Birmingham area were switched on on 31 October 1966. Full electric working from Euston to Crewe started on 6 March 1967. At the same time the former Great Western route from London through Birmingham to Shrewsbury was downgraded to carry only local trains, diverted to use Birmingham New Street and Wolverhampton High Level. The 'Pines Express' was not rerouted this time; it was removed.

The last 'Pines' ran on Saturday 4 March 1967. From 6 March travellers from Manchester could leave Piccadilly at 11.03 and change at Birmingham into the 08.30 Newcastle-Poole, and return on the 09.40 Poole-Newcastle, their connection reaching Manchester at 17.13. On Saturday there was still a through train:

| Manchester | d 11.15 | a 15.53 |
| Bournemouth | a 17.35 | d 09.53 |

Bournemouth in 1967 was less railway-minded than it had been only five years before. (And that lady's coat now cost 18 guineas.) The news everyone wanted to hear was how the bypass was progressing. In February BR mounted a publicity drive, partly to drum up business for the forthcoming electric service to London and partly to alert the populace to a new danger, the live 'Juice' rail. The article was headed 'Last 17 Miles Goes Live', for on 27 February the conductor rails from Lymington Junction to Branksome were energised. There was a slight flurry of interest and it was reported that the Blandford & District Trades Council was going to campaign for the reopening of the S&D, which at that time was still intact as far as Blandford. There is no reason to suppose that this was serious, and BR would not have taken any notice if it had been. On the whole, the commercial interest of the region dismissed the railway and its improvements as 'too slow and too late'. On 4 March a headline appeared: 'Pines Express "steams" north for last time.' It was not on the front page of the *Echo* but back on page 14, the place for minor obituaries.

Below:
The last northbound 'Pines' on 4 March 1967 was hauled by No D1700, which worked south the previous day. At Banbury it is attracting little attention; but most enthusiasts were more interested in various last steam workings elsewhere on that weekend.
K. P. Lawrence

Journeying Through the Heart of England

Portrait of the Pines Express

The route of the 'Pines' embodies a wealth of railway interest and historical association. We will start by summarising the origins of the railway lines, beginning with Manchester to Heaton Norris, the third railway in Manchester. It was the first part of the Manchester & Birmingham Railway, opened on 4 June 1840. Its terminus was initially by Travis Street until a permanent station at Store Street (later called London Road, now Piccadilly) was completed in May 1842. Heaton Norris was the station for Stockport until the great viaduct across the Mersey Valley was ready in December. On 10 May 1842 the line was opened to Sandbach, and by 10 August it made connection with the Grand Junction Railway at Crewe.

Liverpool portions ran past the historic buildings of Edge Hill, dating from 1836 when the original Liverpool & Manchester terminus at Crown Street was replaced by Lime Street. Diverging from the 1830 line just east of Edge Hill, the new line, brought into use on 15 August 1836, descended at 1 in 93 through a tunnel. Rope haulage was used until 1870. During the 1880s the tunnel was opened into a cutting to accommodate four tracks. The first modern marshalling yard, then called the Gridiron, was built near Edge Hill in 1882. The Widnes-Garston branch was opened on 1 July 1852, and a connection from Edge Hill to Speke Junction on the branch opened on 15 February 1864. With the completion of Runcorn Bridge on 1 April 1869, Ditton was linked to Dutton (the junction was named Weaver to avoid confusion) on the Grand Junction main line.

The Grand Junction, notable among the early lines for the lack of fuss with which it came into being, was opened throughout from Warrington to Birmingham on 4 July 1837. Its southern end, through Bescot and Aston to a terminus in Curzon Street alongside that of the London & Birmingham, was largely eclipsed by the Stour Valley route and by the 1920s the 'Pines' was the only passenger train regularly scheduled over its entire length. The Stour Valley line, connecting Wolverhampton directly with Birmingham, was promoted jointly with the Shrewsbury & Birmingham Railway, but the partners fell out and the completed works lay unused for a year before trains began running into its terminus at New Street on 1 July 1852. The three companies mentioned merged in 1846 to form the London & North Western Railway, which thus had three Birmingham termini. It was able to concentrate its services on New Street when the steeply graded link line from Curzon Street Grand Junction was completed in 1854.

Walsall station lay on the South Staffordshire Railway, opened from Bescot on the Grand Junction on 1 November 1847 to a temporary terminus, the permanent station coming into use on 9 April 1849. The curve from Darlaston to Pleck Junction used by the 'Pines' was not built until 1881. The Midland route from Walsall round to Castle Bromwich opened on 1 July 1879, and caused a public outcry when it was approved because it cut through the beauty spot of Sutton Park.

The route south of Birmingham was all part of the Midland empire. The Birmingham & Gloucester was one of the earliest main lines, completed from Cheltenham to Bromsgrove on 24 June 1840, to Cofton Farm (near the later Longbridge car factory) on 17 September and on 17 December to a terminus in Camp Hill which later,

PINES EXPRESS ROUTES

47

like most such termini, became a goods station. From 17 August 1841 its trains ran into Curzon Street by a link onto the London & Birmingham at Grand Junction. From its opening this was the first company to use the Edmundson card railway ticket. At the same time, approaching from the northeast was the Birmingham & Derby Junction, one of the companies which George Hudson welded into the Midland Railway, extended from Whitacre to its own terminus, Lawley Street, on 10 February 1842. The story of how the Midland took over the Birmingham & Gloucester is one of the classics of industrial power politics. The latter, together with its close companion the Bristol & Gloucester, lying between two expansionist giants, the Great Western and the Midland, was being eyed by both of them; indeed, in early 1845 it was negotiating a lease to the

GWR. Two of its directors were travelling to Paddington for a meeting when they chanced to meet John Ellis, Deputy Chairman of the Midland Railway. Ellis offered to better the GWR terms, the three shook hands on a deal on the spot and by 8 February it was signed and sealed.

Passenger trains from the Derby direction were also diverted into Curzon Street in 1851. Through running from northeast to southwest without reversal was made possible by the link from Landor Street Junction to St Andrew's Junction, opened in 1864.

The line which enabled Midland trains to run through New Street without reversing, the Birmingham West Suburban Railway, was built as a branch from Lifford to Granville Street; it opened 3 April 1876. Converting it to double track and linking it to New Street was a costly task, taking two years and being completed in 1885.

The route via Stoke-on-Trent employed the lines of that most vibrant and successful locally-based company, the North Staffordshire Railway. Its main lines were all built within three years of its 1846 Act of Parliament: Norton Bridge to Stoke by 3 April 1848, Stoke to Congleton by 9 October 1848, and Congleton to Macclesfield by 13 June 1849. At Macclesfield it connected with the Manchester & Birmingham branch from Cheadle Hulme, opened on 24 November 1845.

From Gloucester to Cheltenham is the oldest part of the 'Pines' route, opened in 1810. It was then a 3ft 6in gauge tramway and was completely rebuilt by the

Below:
Manchester London Road station midway through its reconstruction in 1960. The main overall roof is partly refurbished and men can be seen working at platform level below the unfinished arch. To the right is the MSJA station, with a diesel train passing behind a water-tower which provided hydraulic power for capstan working in the low-level sidings. Beyond that is Mayfield station. In Fairfield Street is a trolleybus. On the far pavement, two of the trolley-wire poles still show black and white stripes; this was a wartime application following complaints of people walking into street furniture in the blackout. The camera is looking east towards Ashton. *British Railways, LMR*

CREWE

Above:
Liverpool Lime Street station was a cavernous place, the effect enhanced by the rock cutting approach. The original tunnel from Edge Hill was opened out into a series of long bridges or short tunnels, this being the first under Bronte Street. The small tunnel on the left was added as an afterthought to give the station a shunting neck. British Railways, LMR

Birmingham & Gloucester for connection to its main line, reopening as a standard gauge line on 4 November 1840. A fragment remained, crossing the new line outside Gloucester, commemorated in the name of Tramway Junction. The Bristol & Gloucester was also a rebuild of an earlier mineral tramway, opened on 6 August 1835. It was upgraded and converted to broad gauge in 1844 and, as a result of the Midland takeover, was the only major broad gauge railway never controlled by the Great Western. The branch from Mangotsfield to Bath was completed on 4 August 1869; the present station at Bath (Queen Square) opened on 7 May 1870. The link between North and South Junctions at Mangotsfield was taken out of use on 18 September 1962 after through trains were withdrawn, and the Bath branch was closed to passenger trains on 7 March 1966.

The Somerset & Dorset is described as one of Britain's best-loved railways (although that love was not expressed in overwhelming ticket sales), perhaps because of its local origins and its independence. Its

49

Above:
Mossley Hill, the Liverpool station where
expresses stopped to pick up, was rebuilt
along with the electrification project. In
contrast to the dilapidated wooden
buildings and sagging canopies that stood
here before, the new structures were airy
and cheerful. *British Railways, LMR*

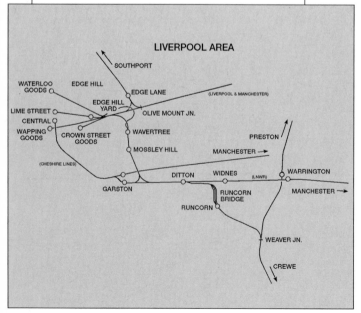

LIVERPOOL AREA

SOUTHPORT

WATERLOO
GOODS

EDGE HILL

EDGE LANE

(LIVERPOOL & MANCHESTER)

LIME STREET

EDGE HILL
YARD

OLIVE MOUNT JN.

CENTRAL

WAPPING
GOODS

CROWN STREET
GOODS

WAVERTREE

PRESTON

MOSSLEY HILL

MANCHESTER →

(CHESHIRE LINES)

DITTON

WIDNES

(LNWR)

WARRINGTON

GARSTON

RUNCORN
BRIDGE

MANCHESTER →

RUNCORN

WEAVER JN.

CREWE

founder was James Clark of Street, brother of
Cyrus Clark of shoemaking fame. Two
nominally independent companies, the
Somerset Central and the Dorset Central,
amalgamated during construction of the line.
It was intended to provide an overland link
from Burnham on the Bristol Channel to
Poole on the South Coast — a logical enough
idea but port-to-port railways have never
prospered in Britain, as in practice the need
is to connect centres of commerce to the
ports. This the S&D discovered, hence its
heroic driving of an extension to Bath, which
broke the company financially and led to its
takeover jointly by the London & South
Western and Midland Railways. The
completion dates were: Wimborne-Blandford
1 November 1860 (the first section to open
for business), Blandford-Templecombe
31 August 1863, Templecombe-Glastonbury
3 February 1862, Evercreech Junction-Bath Junction 20
July 1874, Corfe Mullen Junction-Broadstone 14
December 1885, Broadstone-Poole 2 December 1872,
Poole-Bournemouth West 15 June 1874.

The Somerset & Dorset Joint Committee managed
the line from 1875 to 1947, although from 1930 the
locomotives and operating staff were run directly by the
LMS, while the Southern handled the civil engineering.
Until 1962 much of the management was still separate
from either of the parent regions, and this self-contained
continuity was largely responsible for the special
ambience of the S&D.

Turning now to the 1962 route, Nantwich-Market
Drayton opened on 20 October
1863 and Market Drayton-Wellington on
16 October 1867, these two being independent
companies immediately absorbed by the
GWR. This route was closed to passenger
traffic on 9 September 1963 (to goods on 8
May 1967), so the 'Pines' had to switch to
the Crewe-Shrewsbury branch, built by the
LNWR earlier (1 September 1858). The
Shrewsbury-Oakengates section was unusual
in being half-owned by a canal which had
decided to take up railway building, the
Shropshire Union Railways & Canal Co. (If
that sounds over-optimistic, remember the
venture of the Bristol Tramways & Wagon Co
to diversify into building aeroplanes.) The
other half-owner was the Shrewsbury &
Birmingham, which extended the line to
Wolverhampton on 12 November 1849. It
then used the High Level station but owing
to its disputes with the LNWR it elected to
share the Low Level station of the Oxford,
Worcester & Wolverhampton, which opened
on 1 July 1854. The short connection from
Stafford Road Junction to Cannock Road
Junction opened on 14 November 1854, on
the same day as the line from Priestfield to
Birmingham Snow Hill.

The Oxford-Birmingham line was completed in two stages: to Banbury in 1850 and the remainder on 1 October 1852. It joined end-on with the Great Western's Didcot-Oxford branch of 12 June 1844. The short stretch of the Great Western main line which the 'Pines' used, from Didcot to Reading, dated from 20 July 1840, and the Basingstoke branch, originally broad gauge with its own terminus in Basingstoke, from 1 November 1848.

This takes us to another early main line, the London & Southampton, completed from Southampton to Winchester on 10 June 1839 and from Basingstoke to Winchester on 11 May 1840. Its Southampton station was the one later called Terminus, and into the same came the Southampton & Dorchester Railway on 29 July 1847; all trains reversed there until 1858. The adaptation of that line to serve Bournemouth has already been described.

Lastly, the through route from Cheltenham to Southampton was created by two companies, the Swindon & Cheltenham Extension and the Swindon, Marlborough & Andover; both opened on 5 February 1883 and in 1884 amalgamated to become the Midland

Left:
Runcorn Bridge; a familiar picture, but still the best as it shows the scene before a road bridge was built close alongside. It is taken from the north shore. This is a 'recent' print from a photograph taken in about 1905. *LMSR*

Below:
The Harecastle deviation, used by the 1990s 'Pines', was completed in June 1966, in time to be sullied by steam. On 2 July a train of empty coaches from Llandudno to Stoke, hauled by Class 5 No 45156 *Ayrshire Yeomanry* and Class 9 No 92078, climbs past the Ashnough Reservoir. *M. S. Welch*

& South Western Junction. This company had running powers over the LSWR's Andover-Redbridge branch, known as the Sprat & Winkle Line, completed on 6 March 1865.

The Journey

If we look at a map, the route from Manchester to Bournemouth via Bath is, overall, fairly direct. The distance of 249 miles compares with about 242 by road.

Manchester London Road was built, like many stations close to rivers, entirely on arches in order to ease the approach gradient. There was a large forecourt bridging over Store Street. Beneath it a warren of stores and offices was entered from Store Street, including staff rooms and even a rifle range — important in a country like England where every fit man was liable to be impressed for military service. In this area, and in a goods yard between Travis Street and Walter Street, wagons were moved by capstan and access from the main lines was by three lifts. Two more goods stations lay between Store Street and Ducie Street. Lower still, banished into a tunnel, flowed the Shooters Brook, once a country stream.

The station was in two parts, the LNWR with six platforms and a carriage dock, and the Great Central with three. The approach viaduct carried six tracks, two fast, two slow and two GC; the GC lines were electrified in 1954 on the 1500V overhead system. To the south lay the three-platform station of the Manchester, South Junction & Altrincham line, and south again, entered from Boardman Street, was Mayfield, with three platforms and two docks, built in 1909 as an overflow station because there was no room to expand on the main site. All three were connected by a long footbridge.

Departing trains faced a gradient no worse than 1 in 376 out to Longsight, most of it on arches, and onto the 600yd viaduct over the River Mersey to Stockport Edgeley. The GC line curved away eastwards at Ardwick, and just over half a mile along there were two great railway works, the GC's own and Beyer, Peacock & Co, the firm which exported all over the world and held the rights to the Garratt articulated locomotive.

Stockport was by mid-century joined by continuous building to Manchester, but before that it was of course a market town in its own right, on a hill above the river. The line continued to rise gradually to Alderley Edge, whence there was a similarly gradual fall to Crewe. Once clear of the urban landscape the countryside is rich dairy farming land; indeed, Alderley Edge was a popular resort and the LNWR built a hotel there. East of the line near Goostrey lies the estate of Jodrell Bank, bought by Manchester University, and here in 1957 they built the radio telescope which overlooks the country for miles around, although its own attention is directed far away.

The leaving of Liverpool was a gloomy progress from the cavern of Lime Street station through the walls and arches of the former tunnel up to Edge Hill, amid the sulphur and steam of the labouring engine. Turning sharp right, the climb continued over Mossley Hill, then down to near the Mersey at Allerton. A short run alongside the river, due east, brought you to the lowest Mersey crossing, from Widnes to Runcorn. The curved approach to it lay across a promontory known as Spike Island, which was the port for St Helens where the St Helens Canal entered the river. Here was founded Brunner Mond, the firm which in 1926 became Imperial Chemical Industries. This, one of the key elements of modern civilisation, was founded on salt, the basis for products of which soap, paints, plastics, explosives, bleach, pesticides and glass are just a few.

Runcorn Bridge, designed by William Baker

Pines Route Distances	
	miles chains
Manchester-Crewe	30.70
Liverpool-Crewe	35.50
Manchester-Cheadle Hulme	8.15
Cheadle Hulme-Crewe	22.55
Crewe-Norton Bridge	19.14
Cheadle Hulme-Norton Bridge via Stoke	40.24
Manchester-Norton Bridge via Crewe	50.04
Manchester-Norton Bridge via Stoke	48.49
Norton Bridge-Bushbury	18.79
Bushbury-Birmingham NS via Bescot	16.16
Bushbury-Birmingham NS via Wolverhampton	15.09
Bushbury-Walsall	7.27
Birmingham NS-Kings Norton via Selly Oak	5.41
Birmingham NS-Kings Norton via Camp Hill	7.08
Walsall-Kings Norton	23.43
Bushbury-Kings Norton via Aston	21.57
Bushbury-Kings Norton via Walsall	30.70
Kings Norton-Bath	88.02
Bath-Bournemouth W	71.38
Crewe-Wellington	32.18
Crewe-Wellington via Shrewsbury	42.70
Wellington-Wolverhampton LL	19.46
Wolverhampton LL-Oxford	78.21
Oxford-Bournemouth C	102.26
Bournemouth C-Bournemouth W	3.29
Bournemouth C-Poole	5.58
Manchester-Birmingham NS via Crewe and Wolverhampton	84.12
Manchester-Birmingham NS via Stoke and Bescot	83.64
Manchester-Birmingham SH via Shrewsbury	105.56
Birmingham NS-Bournemouth W via Bath	165.01
Birmingham SH-Bournemouth W via Oxford	171.46
Manchester-Bournemouth W via Wolverhampton and Bath	249.13
Manchester-Bournemouth W via Walsall and Bath	259.33
Manchester-Bournemouth W via Shrewsbury and Oxford	277.22
Cheltenham-Southampton T	96.36
Southampton T-Southampton C	2.31
Liverpool-Southampton C via Cheltenham	230.03
Liverpool-Southampton C via Shrewsbury and Oxford	249.33

and finished in May 1868 after five years' work, has three lattice girder spans, each 305ft long, over the river, and long land viaducts each side. It affords 75ft headroom above high water and above the Manchester Ship Canal, which fortunately fitted under the southern span. The girders are unusual in that they were fabricated *in situ*, and a unique feature is that after electrification the track was laid with ordinary sleepers in ballast. The stonework was finished in a monumental style to dignify the appearance of this dominating structure. It includes a footpath. Just upstream was an unusual device, a transporter bridge: a high girder bridge on which ran a wheeled truck, carrying slung on cables a platform just above the water. The platform carried users between landings on the banks, thus avoiding the need to build high approach roads to achieve a crossing without interference to shipping. It was replaced in 1962 by a massive steel road bridge which made no concessions to appearances.

From Ditton Junction to Sutton Weaver was a hard climb, at 1 in 114, with 1 in 101 through Runcorn station. The Liverpool line came down to Bird's Wood to make a flyover junction with the GJR, by the south end of Preston Brook Tunnel on the Trent & Mersey Canal, although that is not obvious as both railways are in cuttings. The line from here to Crewe was quadrupled just before the war. For some reason the station of Hartford was left with its platforms on the fast lines only, which gave rise to such anomalies as the northbound 'Pines' calling while the southbound did not.

Crewe Works were not visible from the Manchester or Liverpool lines, just the tangle of rails at the junction before entering the rambling station, product of successive enlargements. Had it not been for the wall on the up side and a carriage shed to the south, you would have seen that the station actually lay in open country.

The Grand Junction followed very straightforward country; in fact the steepest gradient on the whole route was the three-mile 1 in 177 down from Whitmore summit northwards, followed by a further three miles at 1 in 269 to Crewe. Descending south from Whitmore, a wooded area of high ground screened the rural scene from the industrial Potteries. The main line passed close to an unannounced branch line, serving a huge secret ordnance factory which

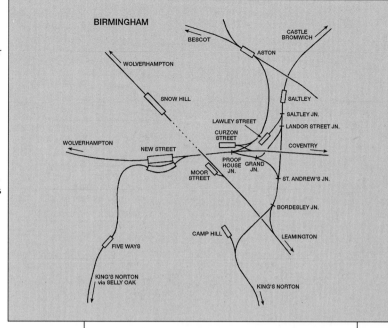

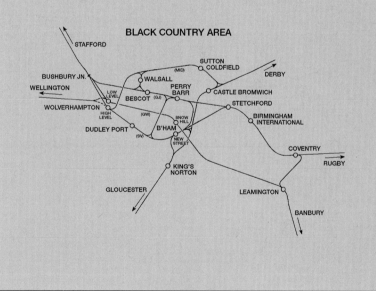

rejoiced in the name of Cold Meece. The Meece Brook, which we crossed near Norton Bridge, was where Izaak Walton wasted his time fishing.

Running into Stafford, the engine-building works of W. G. Bagnall were on the right just north of the station. At the south end the Trent Valley main line curved away to the left, and we took the original line to Bushbury Junction.

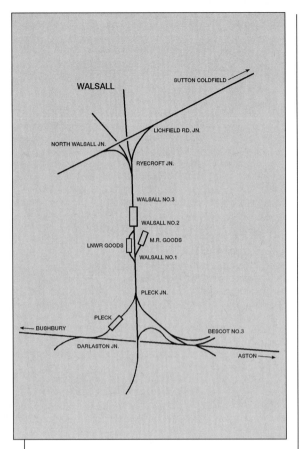

WALSALL

SUTTON COLDFIELD

LICHFIELD RD. JN.

NORTH WALSALL JN.

RYECROFT JN.

WALSALL NO.3

WALSALL NO.2

M.R. GOODS

LNWR GOODS

WALSALL NO.1

PLECK JN.

PLECK

BUSHBURY

BESCOT NO.3

DARLASTON JN.

ASTON

The alternative route from Cheadle Hulme to Norton Bridge via Stoke-on-Trent was in fact 1½miles shorter than that via Crewe, although it seemed longer because of the curves, gradients and variety. It started with a sharp turn and set off at 1 in 191 past Bramhall towards the Pennines. It took a wide curve around the factory of A. V. Roe Ltd at Woodford Aerodrome, whose most famous product was the Avro Lancaster — which was at first called the Manchester. The climb continued for nearly 12 miles to a summit at Macclesfield Moss, then a descent to Congleton. Macclesfield, birthplace of Matthew Pickford and Hovis flour, had two stations close together; Hibel Road was the LNWR and Central the North Staffordshire, the companies making an end-on junction between. Later they were both demolished and replaced by a new station near the site of Central. At Macclesfield the line took company with that remarkable waterway, the Macclesfield Canal, and followed it down to Harecastle Hill. Approaching Kidsgrove, on the left is the sham castle of Mow Cop, built in 1754 by Randle Wilbraham to crown the hill. Incidentally, for those who find the station name of Mow Cop & Scholar Green vaguely familiar although they have never been there, it was one of the names quoted by Michael Flanders in his song *The Slow Train*.

Harecastle Hill forms the northern boundary of the Potteries and was where James Brindley drove the Trent & Mersey Canal through the Central Watershed by a 2,880yd-long tunnel. When started in 1766 it was the largest work of civil engineering yet seen and was regarded with the same awe and incredulity that Box and the Channel Tunnel would arouse in their turns. It took 11 years to complete. In 1824-7 Thomas Telford built a parallel tunnel on its east side, and the railway

Left:
During its last summer, the 'Pines' has arrived at Walsall from Bath behind two Class 5s, the leader being No 44839. They are standing in Platform 1. 'Britannia' No 70004 *William Shakespeare*, gushing steam from her gland packings, departs for Manchester.
J. Haddock

tunnel, to the east again and slightly higher, also took
three years to build and was opened in July 1849. There
were in fact three railway tunnels, one 1 mile 3yd long
and two short ones. When the line was electrified the
tunnels were too small to accommodate the overhead
wires, so a steeply-graded deviation line was built
around the west side of the hill. It came into use on
27 June 1966.

Emerging into a landscape scarred and shaped by
innumerable mines and quarries, the train ran through
the middle of the Potteries, past the original Wedgwood
works at Etruria, through Stoke and on down the Trent
valley. This line was superbly laid out, with many miles
at a ruling gradient of 1 in 330. From Stone it turned
right on the short connecting line to Norton Bridge.

A 'Pines' routed over the Stour Valley line had a
climb at 1 in 101 from Bushbury to Wolverhampton,
then the railway ran alongside the main line of the
Birmingham Canal Navigations. Between Smethwick
and Soho stations it passed the site where a Boulton &
Watt steam engine, now preserved as the oldest
working engine in the world, was erected in 1779.
Whether by this route or through Bescot, it passed
among the industries large and small, the basins and
sidings, back-to-back housing and scorched earth of the
Black Country. The Bescot route was more pleasant, as
some parts of the Tame Valley were still quite rural,
where opposite Hamstead Colliery the owners would

Above:
A 'Britannia' departing from the south end of
Walsall station to Manchester with the
northbound 'Pines'. So filthy as to be almost
beyond identification, No 70022 *Tornado* is
recognisable as an ex-Western Region engine
by the absence of a handrail on the exhaust-
deflector plate. Visible are No 2 signalbox and
the Midland goods station. *J. Haddock*

play golf. Bescot was a large freight marshalling yard, at
the south end of which the line passed under the Tame
Valley Canal. Canals are the main feature of Birmingham,
for it was the only city in Britain, if not in Europe, that
was not founded on a navigable river. It remained an
accretion of villages whose craftsmen made easily
portable products such as needles, knives and guns,
until the waterway network enabled it to exploit the
minerals beneath it. (It is said that Birmingham has
more canal mileage than Venice, which is not quite true
as Venice has no canals.)

If taking the Walsall diversion, you were switched
onto a sharp curve from Darlaston Junction to Pleck
station, round to Pleck Junction and past the goods
yards to stop in Walsall station. Here the replacement
engine would be found waiting in the north bay

Top:

The Midland Railway station at Kings Norton, built in the usual substantial style of that company, with characteristic transverse-ridged canopies, seen in 1969. *A. Muckley*

Above:

At Gloucester Eastgate station on 12 September 1953. The northbound 'Pines' is hauled by 'Royal Scot' No 46122 *Royal Ulster Rifleman*. Across the picture runs the long footbridge linking Eastgate to the GW station, and beneath it on the right are coaches berthed in the original Midland station. *IAL*

platform, having earlier come down by the other side of the triangle from Bescot. The plethora of junctions at each end of the station gave rise to a code of whistles to be used by drivers to declare where they wanted to go, but another order stated that drivers of passenger trains must not whistle before starting. So we would make a furtive departure. At this point the train was heading about north-north-east, Bath being in exactly the opposite direction. It continued thus through the town to Ryecroft Junction, the signalbox which claimed to be the only one controlling four distinct diverging routes. The 'Pines' turned right to join the Midland's Wolverhampton branch at Lichfield Road Junction. This was the line passing through Sutton Park, although the passenger could not appreciate it as the track was mostly in cutting. The park was Birmingham's principal open space; having rail connection was useful for such occasions as the Boy Scouts' International Jamboree in August 1957, when 130 special trains were put on.

New Street station, burrowed into the side of the hill on which stands the cathedral and city centre of Birmingham, was a gloomy place, with tunnels at either

The train swung round onto the Derby line at Castle Bromwich, to enter Birmingham from the northeast. It ran along the south side of the airfield and the wartime factory which produced 11,694 Spitfires. On the other side were Washwood Heath marshalling yard and the works of Metropolitan Cammell.

end, a great cavern filled with the sulphurous miasma of the steam engine. There were actually two stations, the LNWR one, opened in 1854, on the north side and the southern one opened on 9 February 1885 for the use of the Midland. Great Queen Street was enclosed between the two but remained a public highway. Both stations had overall roofs but the LNWR one was removed by the Luftwaffe in 1940 and replaced by unaesthetic platform coverings. After rebuilding in 1962, with a shopping centre on top of it, it became in effect a gigantic underground station. The exit through the tunnels of the Birmingham West Suburban Railway was particularly Dantean, with the engine blasting up the 1 in 80 bank through five short tunnels to Church Road. It was equally difficult to get up to Monument Lane, at 1 in 115, or to Proof House Junction where there was a short incline at 1 in 51. Trains coming in from Bescot faced two inclines, at 1 in 60 to Proof House Junction and 1 in 58 through a tunnel into New Street, and drivers were instructed to stop at Vauxhall unless they had a clear road into the station.

The BWSR was built on the side of the Worcester & Birmingham Canal. Also on the canalside was Bournville, a company town, built by the brothers Cadbury to house the workers of their chocolate factory, which they built in open country in 1879. The factory had a large railway system, its engines noted for their livery which matched the product. The railway followed the canal almost as far as Kings Norton, where the junction with the original main line was realigned in the 1880s.

Below:
On the descent towards Midford, the 'Pines' comes out of Combe Down Tunnel and crosses the short viaduct over the Horsecombe Brook. The viaduct was made to take a double track but the tunnel was not. The 12-coach train is hauled by seven-year-old '9F' No 92001, assisted by 60-year-old Midland 4-4-0 No 40509, in June 1961.
G. F. Heiron

After passing the station there is a view to the right over the canal's Wychall reservoir — it is not generally appreciated that most of the reservoirs in this district were formed to supply the waterway network of the Black Country. A further climb past the Austin motor car works at Longbridge brought you to the pleasant countryside around Barnt Green. Here, near Cofton Farm, there was a tunnel through unstable ground. A 60ft length collapsed on 11 May 1928, killing four men who were working in it, and it was decided to open it out. The 'Pines' was not affected by the operation as it took place on Sunday 27 January 1929, with an Engineers' possession from 10.15pm on Saturday to 6.45am on Monday.

The train made the abrupt plunge from the Midland plateau, down the Lickey Incline, to the basin of the River Severn. At Stoke Works, a plant set up to process the local underground deposits of rock salt, it rejoined the canal and followed it south. However, it avoided the city of Worcester (on the pretext of extortionate land prices when it was built), striking off south through sparsely populated farmland, and for many years the 12½miles from Stoke Works to Wadborough formed the longest section between passenger stations in the country.

Fast running was the rule on the favourable gradients to Ashchurch. Defford Airfield, on the right, was the base, then top secret, of radar test flying during World War 2. Immediately past Defford station the line crossed the River Avon to Eckington, with Bredon Hill on the skyline on the left. A steady gradient of 1 in 300 up was required to take it to Cheltenham, below the western edge of the Cotswold Hills. The Midland station at Cheltenham was Lansdown, on a curve just north of Lansdown Junction, where the GW line went straight on to its terminus of St James. When the GW built its Cheltenham-Stratford line another station, Malvern Road, was added, making three stations within a mile.

The joint line from Cheltenham to Gloucester was widened to four tracks as late as 1942, as a consequence of the local expansion of defence-based industries; a trend which continued after the war with firms exploiting the new profits to be had from electronics. Halfway along it passes another site featured in the annals of 20th-century history, Staverton Airfield, where the first British jet aircraft flight took place in 1941.

Below:
A northbound express on 19 June 1954, at Morewood Colliery Sidings. At this point there is a short level piece, then the descent resumes at 1 in 55. 4-4-0 No 40700 was the last LMS Class 2 built, in 1932. The train engine is Standard Class 5 No 73052. *R. E. Toop*

Above:
Radstock station, looking west, towards Bournemouth, with the level crossing over the main road. *A. Muckley*

Right:
Midsomer Norton station was not exceptional in its structures or facilities, but the staff made it into a showpiece with flowerbeds, tubs and baskets. The platform-sited signalbox with its stone base added to the ambience. In this view there is no sign of life but a barrow-load of boxes is ready to load onto the next up train. *A. Muckley*

MIDSOMER NORTON

SOUTH

Above:
One of Templecombe's Class 4s, No 75004, starting away from Broadstone with the 5.30pm Bournemouth-Templecombe stopping train on Saturday 31 March 1962.
M. J. Fox

Left:
Bournemouth West station on Tuesday 5 July 1938. 'Black Five' No 5272 starts the 3.45pm to Bath; to her left is 'Lord Nelson' No 862 *Lord Collingwood* on the 'Bournemouth Belle', due out at 4.35; on the right the 4.25pm push-pull over the 'Old Road' to Brockenhurst is just visible. Some old LSWR coaches are berthed in the siding on the far right.
IAL/F. E. Box collection

On the outskirts of Gloucester the GW and Midland parted company, the former going straight on and the latter curving to the right, to cross the GW Chepstow line on the level at Tramway Junction and enter Eastgate station. The arrangement at Gloucester was a ridiculous tangle which was never sorted out; GW trains from the Swindon direction could not enter either their own station or Eastgate without reversing. Southwards, two separate double-track lines ran parallel to Standish, where the GW climbed away towards the Cotswolds and the Midland stayed down in the Severn Valley.

Berkeley Road was the junction for Sharpness Docks and the Severn Bridge. The reason for the ascent from there to Yate Court, with five miles at 1 in 270, was not to exhaust firemen at the end of their trip from Birmingham but to reach the mines and quarries, to serve which the railway was built in the first place. On the bank is Wickwar Tunnel, 1,400yd long; its southern half is bored through solid limestone and is unlined.

From Mangotsfield the Bath branch descended on a ruling gradient of 1 in 121 into the Avon Valley. At the bottom it crossed the first of six bridges over the river. At the second bridge, in Saltford, lay a station called Kelston, to distinguish it from the station on the GW

Bristol-Bath line a few yards away. The two lines ran parallel for four miles into Bath. The approach to that noble city was past the gasworks, where the Somerset & Dorset line came in from the right; the locomotive depot was on the left and the goods yard on the right, then over the last Avon Bridge into Queen Square station — renamed Green Park by British Railways.

Bath station's dignified building and splendid overall roof were grandiose for the modest two-platform terminus; very grand for the end of a branch and clearly designed with the S&D extension in mind and with an eye to posterity and future potential. It stands as a reminder of that potential. As the 'Pines' ran in, it

Below:
Aynho station in the Cherwell Valley had a beautiful set of Brunel stone buildings. The wide 'six-foot way' between the platforms shows that it was built on the broad gauge. It lay just south of the junction of the 'New Line' to London, which can be seen going across the background. The train is the York-Bournemouth on 31 July 1956, hauled by No 5981 *Frensham Hall. H. Gordon Tidey*

crossed to the southern platform, and those passengers who troubled to look out would see an engine, or in summer two engines, waiting on the middle road. In the holiday season there would be no point in allowing the children to get out to see them, for they were off the platform end over the river, and in any case there was only a five-minute halt before we were off again. Those engines had to be perfectly prepared with full heads of steam and their fires exactly right for what was to come. On taking the points at Bath Junction they were straight away into a 1 in 50 gradient, on a continuous 20-chain radius curve.

Below:
Lyndhurst Road station was surprisingly rural even as late as 1966 (as was Beaulieu Road), considering that over half a million people lived within a few miles of it. The train is the up 'Bournemouth Belle'. The notice on the gate reads 'Shut this gate to prevent animals straying'. *J. H. Bird*

The S&D ascended the South Down on what was then the edge of the city, although by the time the line closed the whole area had been built over for several square miles. Now heading in almost the opposite direction from when it left the station, it passed through the ridge which carries the main road south, by means of the 447yd Devonshire Tunnel, emerged into a little valley and veered left into Combe Down Tunnel. At the tunnel entrance the gradient reversed to 1 in 100 down. It was to the northbound trains that this tunnel, just over a mile long, was such an ordeal, coming after the heavy work over the Mendips; the engine low on coal, the fireman flagging but having to keep feeding a possibly dirty fire as the confined space of the single-line bore enclosed the engine and all its smoke and steam in a seemingly interminable black hole. Coming out of the south end the engine crew could see ahead into the steep valley of the Midford Brook. The train careered down below the grounds of Midford Castle to the picturesque little station and the viaduct, which in its 168yd crossed above a road, the derelict Somerset Coal Canal, the Cam Brook and the GW Camerton branch.

Above:
Inside Bournemouth Central station on the morning of
16 October 1965, with the 08.34 from Weymouth just
arrived. To augment the two through platforms, the down
platform was lengthened to take two trains and extends
round the bend out of sight. *M. J. Fox*

At this point the line became double, the points
being in the middle of the viaduct, which was built wide
enough for two tracks. It climbed at 1 in 60 above the
Wellow Brook, on a series of reverse curves and
reversals of gradient, a legacy of the early tramway
whose site it occupied. This was a coal area, the biggest
collieries being Braysdown, Writhlington, Radstock,
Kilmersdon and Norton Hill. Just south of Shoscombe &
Single Hill Halt was a short cutting, and beyond that
was the site of the illicit signal cabin called Foxcote,
notorious for the S&D's only major disaster.

Radstock had a large railway complex, two stations
(S&D North, GW South) lying side by side with the
Wellow Brook between them and at the west end two
level crossings on the main road. At the east end a
curve linked the two lines through the sidings of
Ludlows Colliery; in the junction fork was a neat little
engine shed housing the colliery shunters. The latter
were three small saddle tanks constructed at Highbridge
Works, replaced in 1929 by two Sentinel vertical-boiler
engines. Off the platform end at Radstock North was
the start of the big hill; beginning at 1 in 55, easing to 1
in 100 where it crossed over the GW line and the
brook, then at 1 in 50 past Norton Hill Colliery.

Midsomer Norton is such an evocative name that it
is a disappointment to find that the place is a dreary
mining town. The station, however, was delightful,
particularly famed for its gardens. Onwards and
upwards, the 'Pines' climbed into the limestone hills,
beautiful in summer but forbidding in winter when the
west wind drove in from the Bristol Channel with its
load of rain or snow. On the top ridge a Roman road
lies buried beneath the turf where it passed the far older
ramparts of Masbury Castle, a hill-camp. Here in a long
cutting was the railway summit, 811ft above sea level.

The northbound ascent to Masbury from Evercreech
Junction was generally held to be harder, as there were
two three-mile stretches at 1 in 50, broken by a steep
downhill section into the valley of the River Sheppey at
Shepton Mallet. Just south of Charlton Road station the
S&D crossed under another GW branch, from Witham,
and at the same place went under the ancient north-
south highway, the Fosse Way, here adopted as a
modern road. From Cannard's Grave to Evercreech was

a particularly exposed hillside section, then at Evercreech Junction the Bath extension joined the original Somerset Central main line.

The scenery was now exquisitely pastoral, over the River Brue, up to a watershed at Moorhays and into the Blackmore Vale. If you were not going to indulge in the antics at Templecombe (a railway village of the kind found in the north, uncommon in southern England), you would carry on down from No 2 Box, past the goods depot and engine shed on the left; under the Southern main line and out into the fields. The run down the River Stour enchanted you by a succession of names: Sturminster Newton, Stourpaine & Durweston, Charlton on the Hill: in themselves redolent of cider and new-mown hay, but by the same token symbolic of communities that would never make for profitable railway operation. The road was a series of alternating gradients of about 1 in 100 for a few hundred yards, which presented no great obstacles to passenger trains but demanded a high degree of expertise in the driving of loose-coupled freight trains. Near Spetisbury the line was cut through the Iron Age fort called Crawford Castle and the navvies unearthed 130 skeletons, said locally to be corpses from a battle with Romans in the 1st century.

At Corfe Mullen Junction the line forsook the Stour for the hump over Barrow Hill, graded at 1 in 80 on the north side and 1 in 75 on the south side, cutting off the corner round to Broadstone. Leaving the 'Old Road', now hardly used, on the heath, it dropped down to the shore of Holes Bay and followed that into Poole. Here if anywhere was a 19th-century station hopelessly trying to serve the 20th century: on a sharp curve, cutting off

the old town from its developing part, with three level crossings to inconvenience everyone. The 1 in 60 Parkstone bank started on the causeway across Parkstone Bay, with a view out to an expanse of water that was not the open sea but Poole Harbour; the largest natural inlet of its kind in Europe but useless for shipping owing to its negligible depth and shifting sandbanks. Finally, the 'Pines' entered the pine-ornamented residential streets of Branksome and ran down into Bournemouth West. This was an unpretentious terminus, with six platforms and a small goods yard, fronting onto Queens Road. Despite being at the quiet end of town it was a busy place, receiving 74 trains and sending off 60 during a summer Saturday in 1937. Most of the London trains terminated here, together with locals to Salisbury and Brockenhurst via Wimborne and the through trains from up-country. On a Saturday, freight movements went to the main depot at Poole. The 1 in 93 rise straight off the platform ends constituted a test of an engine's sure-footedness, but fortunately most London expresses started with only half a load, to join up with a Weymouth portion at Central. The LMS men from Branksome shed were always happy to turn out to bank any Southern train that got stuck.

Below:
A Bournemouth express emerging from Wickwar Tunnel south end and passing under the aqueduct/footbridge on 21 July 1951. The 12-coach train of prewar LMS stock is hauled by 'Jubilee' No 45569 *Tasmania*. G. J. Jefferson

On the Train

Portrait of the Pines Express

Coaches

Whatever other problems the LMSR faced in becoming a workable entity, its passenger coach policy was never in doubt, for it inherited two schools of coach building which were the best anywhere, those of Wolverton and Derby. With the appointment of R. W. Reid, the Midland Railway's Carriage & Wagon Superintendent, to the same post in the new company, continuity of development of coach design at Derby was assured.

The first coaches built by the LMS were to the latest design evolved by the Midland: 57ft long with an elliptical roof, both of which remained standards for subsequent LMS coaches. The body was of all-wood construction, with a canvas-covered roof. Tare weight tended to increase over the years, from 27 tons to 31 tons for ordinary main-line stock. These coaches were so well built that many of them served until 1968 and they were used on the 'Pines' and similar trains until the

Above:
LMS corridor brake first No 15556, a wood-panelled body with wood and canvas roof, built at Derby in 1929 and scrapped in about 1960. *LMSR*

Left:
Vestibule, or open, third No 9443, a steel-panelled and steel-roof coach built at Derby in 1938 and scrapped in 1966. The livery is simpler than on the 1929 coach, and the ends are painted black instead of crimson. *LMSR*

Above:
Corridor brake third No 26321, a prewar design built in
1945 and scrapped in 1964. Note that you were only
allowed to smoke where it said so. *LMSR*

early 1960s. Indeed, several of their systems, including
the electric lighting, braking and bogie design, were so
advanced that no further change was found necessary.

The Midland coach had the traditional arrangement
of a door to every compartment on the non-corridor
side but by about 1929 the LMS had replaced this by an
arrangement of two windows, one fixed and one
opening. From then on it changed again to having one
large window. The body side profile was flat on the
upper two-thirds and curving inwards on the lower
third, and this again was never changed. There was a
narrow flat panel below the window line, but the
second generation coaches had the window sill lowered
to the top of the curved section, improving the view
out, especially for children. There was also a
constructional change to steel for the body panelling.
The wood panels had raised beading strips to seal the
joins, and these were picked out in elaborate black and
gold lining patterns. The steel panels were larger and
did not need the beading but the painters continued to
apply the pattern, to imitate the appearance of wood
panelling. The Midland body colour of crimson lake was

also used through the 25-year life of the LMS.

In its first and third class accommodation in corridor
trains the LMS aimed to reproduce the level of comfort
expected by its upper-middle and lower-middle class
passengers. (The distinction between the two is roughly
indicated by whether one's domestic servant lived in
the house or came in by the day.) The workshops made
extensive use of prefabricated components, even
complete coach ends being built in jigs to obtain
interchangeability, with the result that the different
types of coaches all had a strong family likeness and the
interior furnishings were largely similar.

With standard parts it was not expensive to produce
many varieties of internal layout. Brake composites were
very numerous; some had two first class and three third
class compartments with a lavatory between them;
some a lavatory, four third compartments, a first
compartment, a first coupé (a half-width compartment
with only one seat) and another lavatory; and some a
third coupé, three third compartments, two first
compartments and the same two lavatories. In the first
and brake first coaches they rang the changes similarly
with compartments, coupés and central or end
lavatories. Third class coaches had seven compartments,
or five compartments and a brake. They seated four a
side, but in the second generation this was changed to
three a side.

The LMS made another break with tradition by building large numbers of open coaches, or vestibule coaches as it called them, and also coaches with half compartments and half open sections. Third vestibules seated 60 passengers in seven and a half bays, the highest capacity of any LMS stock.

The 'Pines' used mainly corridor stock, but additional accommodation put on at busy times would usually be vestibule stock. The 'pre-Pines' was made up of corridor stock with clerestory roofs, as elliptical-roof coaches were not built in quantity until 1921.

The Midland Railway was also responsible for the curious class designation on British railways. What it did on 1 January 1875 was to abolish third class coaches,

but in order to avoid being accused of discriminating against its third-class clientele it called the existing second class 'third', hoping by the way that previous 'second' users might then go 'first'. This anomaly lasted until June 1956, when BR changed third to second.

From 1933 the style of coaches was changed more drastically. Windows were carried in metal frames which were much thinner and entirely concealed behind the body panelling, producing a smooth appearance, and the livery was simplified. The longitudinal wood roof planking was replaced by transverse steel panels. The interiors were given an angular look in keeping with the fashion of the time. A large number of the coaches of this type were built to a 60ft length, increased again to

Left:
A first class compartment in an LMS coach of 1928, one of the first-generation type which retained the Midland windows, one fixed and one opening. *LMSR*

Below:
By contrast, a postwar third class compartment looks pretty austere, although some of the fittings are the same. On this occasion the photographer scorned to put up a scenic view outside the window. *LMSR*

62ft for the brake composites in order to provide more baggage space.

Between the wars a few coaches with all-steel bodies appeared on the LMS, mostly offered by outside contractors, but only after World War 2 did the company start building steel-framed vehicles in its own works. In these the timber body framing was replaced by a structure of steel channel, attached directly to the underframe. It was welded throughout and the panelling was riveted on. These coaches were distinguished externally by a circular window to the lavatory compartment. Some of them were built under BR management in 1948-50 and were painted from new in the BR red & cream colours, but, like much equipment built at this time, they had short lives and were mostly swept away in the changes around the year 1967; changes which included the demise of the 'Pines'.

The services which BR derisorily termed 'cross-country' did not see the new Standard coaches in any numbers until over 10 years after Nationalisation. These vehicles combined the best design and construction practice inherited from the four companies. They were of all-steel, all-welded construction like the last batches of LMS stock, but were longer, based on a 63ft 6in underframe.

They were very strong; a rigid structure permitted larger windows, giving the interiors a light, spacious aspect. The extra length enabled them to do away with that rather claustrophobic feature of LMS corridor stock, the half-compartment. From the passengers' viewpoint however, they looked like the 'austerity' era made permanent, for the BR opinion that the average period of occupancy of a main-line coach was 2hr sat uneasily with the reality of a 7hr journey from the Midlands to the South Coast. The seats were harder and their geometrically patterned upholstery looked meagre in contrast to the abstracts and flowers on LMS seats. Two other demerits of the standard stock were that the tare weight per passenger carried was high and the heat insulation was poor. A 12-coach set of BR stock was 20-25 tons heavier and 67ft longer than 12 LMS coaches, including a kitchen car in each case. A metal coach is inherently colder than a wooden one, and the 1950s saw a rising demand on the part of the British Public for coaches to be heated to summer temperature levels all the year round. The soaring train heating load became a major headache for the Locomotive Department.

Despite the co-ownership of the Somerset & Dorset with the Southern Railway, Southern stock was not used on the regular through trains, although scratch sets were made up for Saturday-only workings such as the Bournemouth-Bradford. The Liverpool-Southampton service was shared with the Great Western Railway, each company supplying one coach, so each day saw a GWR brake composite at Lime Street station, arriving in the afternoon or departing in the morning on alternate days. After Nationalisation the Sheffield through portion was frequently formed of LNER coaches. During the last 10 years the LMS coaches were gradually eliminated but some remained among the BR stock until the end in 1967.

Below:
Vestibule first No 15665, built in 1926, in BR red and cream livery in the 1950s as No M7447M. The panel beading of the body is visible but the new colour scheme ignores it. Real Photographs

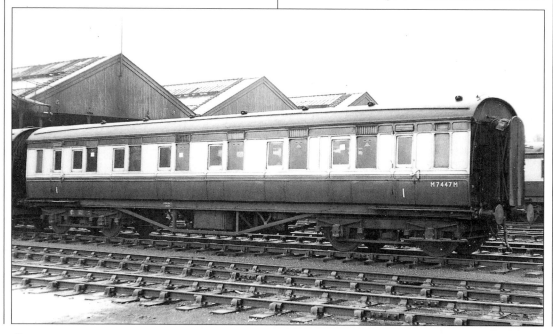

Like many long-distance services, the 'Pines' required two complete trains, each taking two days to make the round trip. The formation varied according to the season. At a minimum, with one coach each for the Liverpool-Bournemouth, Liverpool-Southampton and Bradford-Bournemouth workings and the four-coach Manchester-Bournemouth main train, it mustered only seven coaches. The number increased with demand to a maximum of 12 permitted by its 'Limited Load' classification: typically two Liverpool-Bournemouth, one Liverpool-Southampton, two Bradford-Bournemouth and seven Manchester-Bournemouth. On those days when it stopped in Birmingham to attach or detach the Bradford coaches, there was another portion which ran between Manchester and Birmingham.

The LMS allowed passengers free carriage of luggage up to 100lb for third class and 150lb for first class. In order to provide ample space for it, each portion conveyed at least one brake composite coach, seating typically 12 first and 24 third. When this had to be augmented the favoured companion vehicle was a

Top:
In about 1960 BR issued this publicity view of its new-style dining car interiors. It claimed that 'The colourful furnishings are a complete departure from the usual pattern'. *BR*

Above:
Twelve-wheeled first/third kitchen/dining car No 223, built at Wolverton in 1925, as running in its final years. It was converted to a kitchen/buffet in 1954, also by Wolverton, and scrapped in 1962. *IAL*

PINES EXPRESS TYPICAL TRAIN FORMATIONS

Pre-War

BCK	TK	BCK	RCO	RT	CK	TK	BTK	BCK	TK	BCK
Brad-Bmth				Man-Bmth				Lpl-Bmth		Lpl-Sotn

Pre-War, leaving Manchester

BCK	TK	BCK	BCK	RCO	RT	CK	TK	BTK
Man-Brum			Man-Bmth					

Pre-War, Saturday

BCK	TK	BCK	BCK	RCO	RT	TO	TO	CK	TK	BTK
				Man-Bmth						

1947-50

BTK	CK	BCK	CK	CK	RCO	TO	TO	TO	TK	BTK
Bmth-Shef TWTh / Man-Bmth MFS					Man-Bmth					

1950-62

BTK	CK	BTK	CK	BTK	CO	RT	TO	TO	TK	CK	BCK
Shef-Bmth		Lpl-Bmth				Man-Bmth					

1963-67

BSK	CK	SO	BSK	BSK	SK	SK	SO	RF	SO	CK	BCK
Lpl-Bmth				Man-Bmth							

BCK – brake composite corridor   CK – composite corridor   BSK – brake second corridor
TK – third corridor   BTK – brake third corridor   SO – second open
RCO – dining composite vestibule   TO – third vestibule   SK – second corridor
RT – kitchen/dining third   CO – composite vestibule   RF – kitchen/dining first

56-seat corridor third. In the Manchester portion would be in addition a brake third and one or more corridor thirds and corridor composites.

On summer Saturdays, when there were no Liverpool coaches, their place was taken by further accommodation for Manchester, often using vestibule composites or thirds, to make up the full load, so that such a train had fewer brake vehicles in it.

This was also the situation after the war; portions serving Sheffield and Liverpool ran on weekdays, while on summer Saturdays the whole train was required for Manchester passengers. The growth of travel through the 1950s was such that it was seldom seen with less than the full 12 coaches. In the last phase, after the rerouteing of 1962, there was no Sheffield portion but the Liverpool portion was enlarged to four coaches.

On the main train, running between Manchester and Bournemouth, a full meal service was provided. The formation included a kitchen/third dining or kitchen/first dining car, paired with a first/third dining car or an equivalent combination. Through the 1920s the rostered kitchen cars for the two sets were a Midland Railway first and an LNWR 65ft, 12-wheeled first. In the autumn of 1934 the train received new LMS kitchen/thirds and these served until about 1962. They were massive coaches, with 68ft bodies carried on six-wheel bogies, weighing 45 tons. One of these with a composite dining car could seat 18 first and 48 third class diners. During the 1960s BR kitchen/firsts were used, so that the train could sometimes, though not always, be seen made up entirely of Standard coaches. There was no pre-cooked food; the chef produced the meals from raw ingredients on the day. The kitchen's gas supply was replenished at Birmingham or Walsall during the engine change.

When all these parts were added together, typical specimens of the 'Pines', as seen on the section between Birmingham and Cheltenham, would be made up as in the accompanying diagrams.

Incidentally, the LMS type codes were different from the later BR codes; for example, a vestibule first was designated QL, a brake composite was CBB and a brake third was CH. The BR codes have been used as more readers will be familiar with them.

The formation was laid down in a Passenger Train Marshalling Book, which ordered the types of coaches to be provided, classified by seating accommodation. The staff responsible for carrying out its ordinances had, in theory at least, to

Left:
The happy passengers in this July 1957 picture of a BR Standard open second, are obviously posed, particularly the lady gazing fascinated at the shop floor outside the windows. Above the vestibule door is a small plate stating the wood used for the internal panelling. *BR*

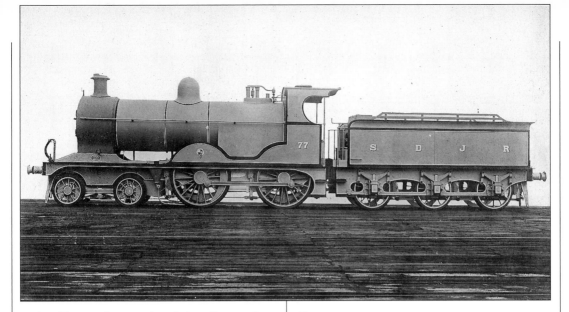

work within two other sets of restrictions. One was the weight of the train. Another book, Loads of Passenger Trains, laid down the load limit for each class of engine on each route; by 'class' is meant not the variety of engine design but the power classification, which on the LMS was on a scale from 1 to 7. British Railways adjusted the scale to read from 1 to 8, and their version is used in the tables here because it is far more widely known. Classes 1 and 8 were not applicable to our interest. The loads always refer to the tare weight, without passengers.

Above:
4-4-0 No 77, built for the S&D. The plate below the smokebox reads, 'Midland Rly Co, Makers, Derby 1907'. In the 1930 amalgamation she was numbered 320, but was scrapped the following year. *IAL/LPC*

The other restrictions related to the length of the train; this had to be limited at some places, mostly terminal stations, where over-long trains would extend not only beyond the platforms but also over pointwork and thus interfere with the normal working of the station. Manchester London Road applied a limit of 11 bogie coaches for incoming trains, and Bournemouth West was limited to 12. Bath Queen Square could only accommodate 9 coaches in its platform, but longer trains could be handled. Birmingham New Street could take 15. Liverpool Lime Street had a limit of 13 and had an additional restriction: an incoming train had to include at least two brake vehicles. This was to ensure adequate brake power when it was subsequently lifted by a shunting engine up the incline out of the station.

After the 1962 rerouteing, the Bournemouth length restriction no longer applied, and 13-coach formations grossing up to 500 tons were permitted. The first southbound train via Oxford had 13 on. The load limit for electric locomotives, north of Crewe, was 500 tons, and for diesel locomotives was 475 tons. The latter was raised to 525 tons for the Brush D1500 series locomotives.

For a train encompassing such variations as did the 'Pines', this plethora of limits could be a source of controversy. A foreman at Edge Hill, forced to replace a defective coach at short notice, might not be able or willing to take account of the circumstance that the coaches already on the way from Bradford would cause

Load Limits (in tons) on 'Pines' Route

Midland Lines, 1954

Engine class	2	3	4	5	6	7
Birmingham-Blackwell via Selly Oak	220	260	280	345	385	420
(when banked to Church Road Jn)				300	365	405
Blackwell-Bristol	240	290	320	370	400	480
Bristol-Birmingham	240	290	320	370	400	480
Saltley/Birmingham-Kings Norton via Camp Hill	225	270	300	345	390	450
Kings Norton-Saltley/Birmingham via Camp Hill	240	290	320	370	415	480
Walsall-Castle Bromwich	-	-	-	360	380	-
Castle Bromwich-Walsall	200	245	270	310	350	-
Castle Bromwich-Saltley	240	290	320	370	415	480
Mangotsfield-Bath	270	325	360	415	470	-
Bath-Mangotsfield	230	280	310	355	405	-

The S&D was of course a law unto itself, and the following list applied in the prewar period:

	Bath-Evercreech	Evercreech-Corfe Mullen
S&D 5ft9in 4-4-0	160	290
S&D 6ft 4-4-0	170	290
Midland 7ft 4-4-0	190	290
LMS Class 2 4-4-0	210	290
LMS Class 4 0-6-0	240	365
LMS Class 5 4-6-0	270	405
LMS Class 7 2-8-0	315	450

his chosen substitute to put the train over weight. Before each run the load was telephoned to the locomotive depot, and if it was over the limit for the engine, a second engine and crew should be turned out. In reality, railwaymen were often willing to stretch the point, but they were always concerned that a special effort be not taken by the management as something that could be demanded every time.

Locomotives — from Two to Nine

R. M. Deeley of the Midland Railway introduced a table of power classification numbers, which with slight alteration was continued by the LMS and BR.

Class 2 and 3

The 'pre-Pines' and other north-south through trains were normally hauled by Midland four-coupled bogie express engines. These and their LMS successors were used on the 'Pines' itself during its first decade, and came on to the front of it to assist a younger engine on the climb over the Mendips until 1961.

Derby Works did not give engines class designations; they built engines in batches and identification was by running number, or by coupled wheel diameter and cylinder size. The 4-4-0 type was introduced by Samuel Waite Johnson, Locomotive Superintendent from 1873 to 1903. The first, No 1312, with 17½in by 26in cylinders and 6ft 6in wheels, was built by Kitson & Co of Leeds in 1876. Various wheel sizes up to 7ft were employed, and all had round-topped fireboxes and slide valves until 1896, when Belpaire fireboxes and piston valves were adopted. Grate area ranged from 17 to 21sq ft. They were given

Left:
A Midland 4-4-0, one of the last Class 2s, built in 1901, seen as rebuilt under Henry Fowler about 1912. This engine survived until 1959. *IAL/LPC*

Left:
Similar in nearly all respects to the Midland design, an LMS Class 2 4-4-0 (one obvious difference is being driven from the left). No 40564 was the second built, in 1928. In her last year she was considered good enough to assist the 'Pines', and is seen starting northwards from Shepton Mallet on 29 March 1961. It is likely that the crew put some coal dust on the fire to produce a smokescreen for the photographer. The train engine is Class 5 No 73047. *G. Richardson*

Above:
The first Midland Compound, standing at
Derby Works on 28 July 1959 after restoration to
working order. She is as rebuilt in 1914. *G. Wheeler*

Class 2 by Deeley; larger ones built from 1900 to 1905
were classed 3. About 350 were built; rebuilt at least
twice, with larger superheater boilers; 190 were taken
into BR stock in 1948 and the last, No 152 of 1899, BR
No 40537, was scrapped in 1961. The LMS built 138
basically similar engines, with 19in cylinders and 6ft 9in
wheels, during the years 1928 to 1932. All Midland
engines were driven from the right-hand side of the
footplate, whereas the LMS adopted the LNWR left-
hand drive.

Johnson was one of the foremost railway engineers
of his time, a member of the Institution of Civil
Engineers, President of the Institution of Mechanical
Engineers and Founding Chairman of the Association of
Railway Locomotive Engineers. He would not have been
so highly regarded if his designs had been, as some
later commentators have alleged, inadequate. The
Midland had a policy of running light, fast and frequent
trains, believing that a short train every hour was a
better service than a long one every 2hr. With the loads
for which they were designed, the Johnson engines
could reach maximum speeds of 90mph and achieve
60mph averages with ease.

Unfortunately, good equipment tends to be well-
used, then mis-used and abused, and finally condemned
as useless for purposes for which it was never intended.
The decision to build Midland designs after the
Grouping was undoubtedly wrong, for they were

unsuited to the conditions then found on the LMS.
Enginemen were obliged to struggle with frames that
were too weak, axle bearings too small, and injectors
that could not keep the boilers full for the work they
were trying to do with them, and thus machines once
acclaimed as the finest in Europe were so much
disparaged in their later years. By the late 1920s,
expresses such as the 'Pines' had to be double-headed
as a general rule.

The Midland assumed responsibility for engines on
the Somerset & Dorset when it and the LSWR took over
the line in 1875, and from 1891 to 1928 supplied 21
4-4-0s for passenger work. (From 1930 the S&D
engines were accounted as part of the LMS stock.) The
first 11 were specially built, the later ones were
standard Midland/LMS engines. The last in service, S&D
No 45, BR No 40634, lasted until 1960. Their 7ft wheels
were no handicap on that steeply graded route, for
wheel size does not in itself affect an engine's ability to
lift a load up a gradient. Provided that the desired
tractive force is available at the wheel rim, the diameter
of wheel producing it is immaterial. Moreover, once it is
under way, a small-wheeled engine is at a

disadvantage, for it turns faster than its large-wheeled sister at the same road speed, and the torque of a steam engine falls off very rapidly with increase in speed.

Class 4

By the time the 'pre-Pines' started in 1910, the top jobs had been turned over to the Midland's most famous engines, the 4-4-0 Compounds.

The principle of compounding is simple to state: steam which has propelled a piston down one cylinder is made to repeat the action in another cylinder, so as to extract more energy from it and make the engine more efficient. It is commonly used in stationary plant and ships, but applying it to a railway engine raises several questions. How to arrange the timing so that the low-pressure cylinder is ready to receive steam from the high-pressure one; this must be compatible with the need to quarter the cranks to avoid dead centres and even out the torque, bearing in mind that heavy flywheels are ruled out. What proportions to adopt for the hp and lp cylinders; how to arrange these different sized cylinders in the engine structure, and how to achieve static and dynamic balancing of the resulting mechanism. A railway engine must start its load from rest, when there is no hp exhaust steam and hence the lp cylinder is useless unless it can be given steam direct from the boiler, which adds complication and expense. And by no means least, the driver, unlike a ship's engineer who is solely devoted to watching the performance of his engine, has many other matters

demanding his attention, like looking where he is going, and should not be given extra tasks such as deciding the relative hp and lp cut-offs to be used.

The Midland system was essentially that devised by W. M. Smith of the North Eastern Railway. It had one 19in hp cylinder between the frames, with piston valves mounted beneath it, and two 21in lp cylinders outside the frames, with slide valves inside the frames behind them. The cut-offs were fixed relative to each other, and were both controlled by one reversing lever. When the regulator was opened, the initial travel of the handle opened what was termed a bypass valve, which

Below:
LMS-built Midland Compounds in Birmingham New Street on 25 October 1957, by which time they were used only on local passenger turns. No 41195 is standing on the siding between Platforms 7 and 8, on the Midland side, and No 41046 is running back through Platform 8. *R. J. Blenkinsop*

Right
BR Standard Classes 4 and 5, Nos 75023 & 73050, getting under way with the 'Pines' on the haul over the Mendips from Evercreech Junction on 10 September 1961. The front of No 75023, then only seven and a half years old, is in a shocking state; water running from the smokebox, ash lying on the deck and collision damage evident on the front corner. But then, steam engines were cheap and expendable. *G. Richardson*

admitted live steam to the receiver between hp and lp cylinders, so the engine started as a two-cylinder simple. (The same live steam also passed into the exhaust side of the hp cylinder, so its piston had equal steam pressure coming in on both sides and thus floated, contributing no effort and actually exerting a braking effect at speed.) It was not ideal, but it worked. When the regulator was pushed over to the full open position, the bypass valve closed and the engine compounded. That led to an unusual driving technique, in that if you wanted more power at low speeds you actually had to partially close the regulator. The lp cranks were quartered in the usual way. The hp crank was at 135° to both. This also was a compromise, for although it was ideally placed to be exhausting as the left-hand lp piston was taking the steam for its stroke, it

was not quite so well timed for the right-hand one. As a result, although the engine has the same four exhaust beats per wheel revolution as a two-cylinder engine (the hp exhaust does not go to the chimney), the beat is slightly irregular when working compound.

The first engine, No 2631, was built at Derby in 1902, followed by four more. They had 7ft wheels and the then high boiler pressure of 195psi. In their original form the lp bypass valve was actuated by a second regulator handle and the hp and lp cut-offs could be altered separately or together by coaxial reverser shafts. Johnson's successor, R. M. Deeley, did away with these complexities and built 40 engines to a similar design in 1905, and the LMS built 195, with 6ft 9in wheels and 200psi superheater boilers, from 1924 to 1930. The grate area of 28½sq ft was the same as the LMS

Class 5MT and the Southern Railway 'Schools' class, which they preceded by some years.

They continued on top-rank express work on the Midland lines until the arrival of the 'Jubilee' 4-6-0s, after which they were gradually downgraded. One was tried on the S&D in 1924 but presumably found wanting, as no more were seen there. However, in late 1939 they were cleared for use, as were the 'Land Crab' 2-6-0s, in anticipation of the more powerful engines being moved elsewhere. In mid-1940 No 1046 was fitted with a single-line tablet catcher and worked on the S&D for the duration of the war, usually on the 10.5am Bath-Bournemouth. A few survived in service until the spring of 1960, the last one running being No 907, and the last two, Nos 936 and 1168, were officially scrapped in October.

The first Compound, renumbered 1000 in 1907, was preserved by BR and hidden in Crewe Works until early in 1959, when she was restored to running order. Until 1962, and again from 1975 to 1983, she hauled special trains. She now appears in the guise to which she was rebuilt in 1914. As the only operational Compound in mainland Britain, she has never received her due share of public attention.

Before the advent of Stanier 4-6-0s, the 'Pines' was usually hauled north of Birmingham by a 'Prince of Wales' 4-6-0 based at Crewe North depot. This very successful type was designed by C. J. Bowen Cooke in 1911 and 246 were built: 20 by the North British Locomotive Co, 90 by the shipbuilders Beardmore on the Clyde and the rest at Crewe. They had 6ft 3in wheels, 20in cylinders and Joy valve gear. They were robustly built in the Crewe tradition, were worked hard and clocked up many miles. The developments of the 1930s caused them to be superseded after short lives, but the national emergency slowed down the pace of replacing them. Fourteen

survived the war and the last, No 25752, was scrapped in July 1949. BR junked a large number of historic engines at this time, an act of vandalism quite comparable with anything that was done later.

Beginning in 1960, a Class 4 of a very different feather appeared on the 'Pines': BR Standard 4-6-0s, based at Templecombe depot, providing assistance between Evercreech Junction and Bath. They included the preserved No 75027.

Class 5

The 1927 publicity drive, with its train names, coincided with the introduction of the 'Royal Scot' class. As they came into use they made for wider availability of the previous most powerful type, the LNWR 'Claughtons'. However, the Class 5 type most associated with the 'Pines' is the 4-6-0 of 1934. It is generally attributed to W. A. Stanier; but although he was a fine practical engineer, his main work was done on the Great Western Railway and by the time he joined the LMS at the beginning of 1932 he was more interested in the business of engineering. For half his time as Chief Mechanical Engineer he was largely an absent figurehead, and credit for the engines of this period should really go to the Chief Draughtsman T. Coleman. Stanier was principally the instrument by which Sir Harold Hartley persuaded the parsimonious LMS Board to invest in large, modern engines in the quantities that were desperately needed. Crewe, Derby, Horwich, the Vulcan Foundry, Sir W. G. Armstrong Whitworth & Co, and North British Locomotive Co built nearly 1,000 in five years. The 4-6-0s came in two varieties; the black ones, Class 5MT, and the red ones, Class 5XP, later called 'Jubilees'. (We will look at the latter under their BR classification of 6.) The first '5MT' delivered was No 5020, from Vulcan, in September 1934.

Left:
'Black Five' No 44847 at Banbury in August 1966, during the last year when the Western Region had dispensed with steam and the LMR was using the depot to service engines on north-south workings.
I. J. Hodson

Left:
'Patriot' No 45505 *The Royal Army Ordnance Corps*, of Longsight, standing at the east end of Platform 9 in New Street, filling the whole place with steam and smoke. She has brought up the 10.15am from Liverpool, which conveyed the 'Pines' portion to Crewe, and is now waiting to take on the northbound 'Pines'. The far platform is the southernmost one in the station and, as the barrow in the doorway shows, adjoins a small parcels loading bay.
M. Mensing

'Black Fives' are of course widely held to be the most successful British steam engines, although it is worth remembering that even they went through three boiler designs in the early years. They and, later, the similar BR Standard version hauled the 'Pines' regularly until 1962. As the train weight crept up during the 1950s it began to exceed their limit and they had to be double-headed, as had the 4-4-0s a generation before.

The S&D was regarded as a severe test of an engine and its men were severe critics. After the bridges between Mangotsfield and Bath had been reinforced to take their weight, 'Black Fives' reached Bath in 1938 and proved an immediate success. The first 'Pines' turn worked was the southbound on 2 May, hauled by No 5440; this engine stayed on the S&D for 20 years.

In the summer of 1954 three new Standard '5s', Nos 73050, 73051 and 73052, arrived at Bath and took over the 'Pines' duty. They and others of this type worked it until 1962.

There was another Stanier Class 5, the 2-6-0 of 1933, used as the guinea pig before commencement of large-scale production. One of these, No 42956, hauled the 'Pines' on 9 August 1958 on the Bath-Birmingham section. For how far is not certain; the record comes from an observer who saw her on the Lickey Incline. A year later No 42968 was similarly noted, not on the actual 'Pines' but on the 8.40am Bournemouth-Bradford of 8 August 1959. These were both Saturdays, when motive power was often in short supply.

The LNER equivalent of the 'Black Five', the 'B1' class, also rates a mention. They were highly regarded by enginemen and if one happened to be on hand when a failure of the booked engine occurred, it would be taken away and be lost to its home depot for another day or two. Nos 61027, 61152 and 61176 were seen on the 'Pines' by means of this process.

A famous engine of another type rated at Class 5, Great Western No 4942 *Maindy Hall*, hauled the 'Pines' from Bournemouth via Salisbury, Westbury and Bristol to Birmingham on 6 December 1960 and back on the next day.

Not the 'Pines' but its companion, the 11am Poole-York, was hauled from Oxford to Banbury on 3 January 1966 by No 6998 *Burton Agnes Hall*, the last passenger duty by a Western Region steam engine.

From 1964, when the Southern Region became chronically short of engines, a Standard '5' sometimes appeared on the Bournemouth-Oxford turn, which was supposed to be taken by a much larger 'Merchant Navy'. By then the long-term consequences of thrashing an engine along with an excessive load no longer mattered.

Class 6

These are the engines which were classed '5XP' by the LMS: the rebuilt 'Claughtons', 'Patriots' and 'Jubilees'. The 'Patriot' was essentially a lighter version of the 'Royal Scot', created to use some parts recovered from scrapped 'Claughtons'. There were originally 130

'Claughtons', of which 42 were nominally rebuilt in this way in 1930-3, and 10 'Patriots' built entirely new in 1934. The 'Jubilee' looked like a 'Patriot' with a '5MT' boiler but differed slightly from both, as the table shows:

	5MT	'Jubilee'	'Patriot'
Cylinders	2: 18½in x 28in	3: 17in x 26in	3: 18in x 26in
Wheels	6ft 0in	6ft 9in	6ft 9in
Grate Area	28½ft²	29½ft²	30½ft²
Boiler Dia	5ft 8½in	5ft 8½ in	5ft 5in
Tube Length	13ft 3in	14ft 3in	14ft
Tubes (small)	151 @ 1⅝in	160 @ 2in	140 @ 2⅛in
Weight	70t 12cwt	80t 15cwt	80t 15cwt

It was unfortunate that the 'Jubilees' were not given the same boiler as the '5MTs', for as built they were indifferent performers, worse than the Midland Compounds which they were supposed to replace. The trouble lay in the boiler: the blastpipe and chimney gave insufficient draught on the fire, and the cross-section area through the superheater was too small, throttling the steam flow. The boiler was redesigned with a larger superheater, smaller blastpipe, greater tube area and larger firebox, after which they were as good as the '5MTs'. They worked all the Midland lines expresses until superseded by diesels.

They were not originally intended to have names, but in 1935, the year of King George V's silver jubilee,

No 5642 was named *Silver Jubilee* and exchanged numbers with 5552, the first of the class, for the purpose of being photographed in patriotic poses. In accordance with the general surge in public flag-waving, more names followed. The themes were states of the Empire, battleships and famous admirals — though seeing, for example, *Anson, Keppel* and *Beatty* in proximity does rather put one in mind of a music-hall act.

The design staff still thought the steam-raising could be improved and designed a larger boiler which fitted the 'Jubilees', 'Royal Scots' and 'Patriots'. Engines with this boiler moved up into Class 7. The first conversion was 'Jubilee' No 5736 *Phoenix* in April 1942, the last was 'Royal Scot' No 6137 *The Prince of Wales's Volunteers (South Lancashire)* in May 1955 but the programme was very desultory and only 91 of the 314 engines were converted.

Class 7

The rebuilt 4-6-0s, comprising 70 'Royal Scots', 18 'Patriots', two 'Jubilees' and the unique No 6170 *British Legion*, were displaced from top link jobs on the London routes by diesels from 1958, and began to appear on the Bristol-Birmingham line. This sometimes brought them onto the 'Pines'; on 10 June 1961 No 46100 *Royal Scot* was seen taking the northbound out of Bath, and No 46115 *Scots Guardsman* worked it on at least one occasion.

In one of the management reshuffles which bedevilled the S&D, responsibility for motive power was changed to the Southern Region in 1950. In March 1951 'West Country' No 34109 *Sir Trafford Leigh-Mallory* was tested on the line and worked the first 'Pines' after the fuel emergency, on 19 March. In May Nos 34040-4 were put on the top turns, including the 'Pines'. This was considered very dashing, and the feature film *The Titfield Thunderbolt*, made in 1953, opened with a view of a 'West Country' sweeping across Midford Viaduct to represent the modern era in contrast to the branch line train chuffing past below. However, the S&D soon teased out two weaknesses in these otherwise very capable engines. They were prone to slipping when climbing the Mendips and to be on a 'West Country' that had lost her feet in Combe Down Tunnel was an uncomfortable, indeed unhealthy, experience. They were also noted for having uncovered boiler lagging above a casing with 40gal of oil sloshing about in it. During the heavy braking on the way down the Mendips, red-hot particles flying off the brake blocks started fires in the oily lagging. The best known incident occurred on the 'Pines' in 1951, when No 34040 *Crewkerne* had to stop at Radstock to be extinguished.

Another snag with 'West Countries' was that they did not carry enough coal. It had become so accepted that engines making the round trip from Bath did not need to refuel that coal provision at Branksome had

disappeared. With only 5 tons on the tender, even leaving Bath shed with the firebox stuffed full and a heap on the cab floor, 'West Countries' when fully loaded often could not manage it and had to go round to Bournemouth Central for more coal to get them back. As a result of these shenanigans they were restricted to the same 270 tons maximum loading as the 'Black Fives', despite being so much more powerful on paper. They were moved away from Bath at the end of 1954 but Bournemouth (Southern) Depot continued to provide 'West Countries' for summer services on the S&D. As late as 6 November 1965, No 34044

Left:
'Jubilee' No 45604 *Ceylon*, of Crewe North, starting a load of empty coaches at Stafford station some time in March 1959. *K. R. Pirt*

Below:
'Royal Scot' No 46137 *The Prince Of Wales' Volunteers (South Lancashire)*, the last to be rebuilt, about to set out from New Street Platform 7 with the 10.5am Bournemouth-Derby on 1 July 1961, with a carriage examiner and the boys on the platform taking their respective interests. It was running half an hour late. The view under the low bridges of Queen's Drive and Worcester Street shows the difficulty and danger of carrying out shunting in this station. *M. Mensing*

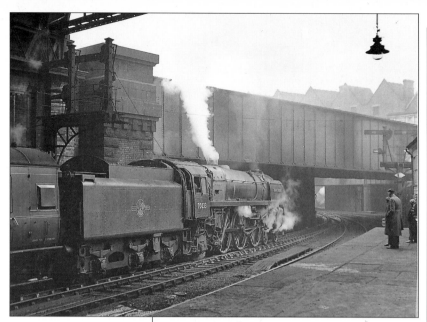

Right:
Another Class 7 engine, BR Standard 'Britannia' No 70033 *Charles Dickens*, built in 1952 and scrapped in 1968, on the northbound 'Pines' in New Street on 8 November 1958, in the lull before departure. *M. Mensing*

Below:
Southern 'West Country' No 34024 *Tamar Valley*, built in 1946 and scrapped in 1967, on the 'Pines' duty in March 1964. Having turned and refuelled at Oxford, she rolls through the station to pick up the southbound train. The engine duty number 399 is on the headcode discs. *I. J. Hodson*

Woolacombe worked the 09.37 Bournemouth-Bath and the 19.55 return.

No 34102 *Lapford* attained notoriety in December 1960, when the train was routed via Salisbury and Bristol. On the 5th she ran through from Bournemouth to Birmingham. On the 6th she came back, but ran out of coal at Downton, with 30 miles to go, and just waffled into Bournemouth at her last gasp. On the 7th No 34043 *Combe Martin* was relieved at Gloucester by Class 5 No 44981.

'West Countries' were the usual power between Bournemouth and Oxford from September 1962 until mid-1966. No 34040, veteran of the S&D days, was on the duty on 17 June 1966. They were still penetrating the Western Region after the demise of the 'Pines';

No 34104 *Bere Alston* worked into Reading on 20 March 1967 and No 34090 *Sir Eustace Missenden* arrived there with the 10.46 from Bournemouth on 1 April.

BR Standard 'Britannia' class 4-6-2s found their way onto the 'Pines' when displaced from more important duties. They included Nos 70004 *William Shakespeare* and 70014 *Iron Duke*, better known for their exploits on the 'Golden Arrow' in Kent.

Also in Class 7, Great Western 'Castles' worked the Wolverhampton-Oxford leg from September 1962 until full diesel working was achieved. Among them was No 7029 *Clun Castle*.

The Somerset & Dorset's peculiar Class 7F 2-8-0s were never rostered for the 'Pines'.

Class 8

LMS Pacifics were never used on the 'Pines' because they were all needed elsewhere and they were not permitted on the routes via Stoke and Walsall.

Shortly after Bournemouth men took over the working to Oxford, they complained that 'West Countries' would not be able to maintain the forthcoming accelerated schedule and it was rostered for a 'Merchant Navy'. This had 29% more grate area (and 74% more than a 'Black Five'!). In fact the smaller engines were perfectly able to time the train but being worked rather harder they actually consumed more coal and water, making more work for the fireman and on a bad day making it tight to get through. In practice, of course, they very often still got a 'West Country' and had to put up with it. This was notable as the only passenger turn regularly worked by a 'Merchant Navy' which was not a London train.

On 29 April 1967 No 35030 *Elder Dempster Lines* became the last steam engine to work a through service to Bournemouth when she took over the Newcastle train from a Brush Type 4 diesel at Reading.

What would have been the most spectacular run with a 4-6-2 regrettably did not happen. The LNER 'A4' No 60024 *Kingfisher* was on the Southern in March 1966 for the A4 Locomotive Society's Weymouth and Exeter railtours of the 26th and 27th, and they booked her to take the northbound 'Pines' on the 29th. Something (unspecified) was found amiss with the engine on the day, and she eventually returned north running light.

Above:
At the north end of Oxford station on 8 August 1964. 'Castle' No 4093 *Dunster Castle*, then 41 years old, has brought in a southbound through train, has run back through the down platform and is waiting to be switched into the shed. 'West Country' No 34103 *Calstock*, then 14 years old, has arrived on a holiday extra from Bournemouth to Kidsgrove (Stoke-on-Trent), which she worked forward. Both engines are standing on a bridge over a water link from the Thames to the Oxford Canal. *S. Creer*

Class 9

This brings us to the episode, brief as it was, for which the 'Pines' is best known: the three glorious summers of the '9F' 2-10-0s.

The whole thing came about by the merest accident. The committee set up by the British Transport Commission's Railway Executive to design the Standard engines did not think it necessary to include any dedicated freight engines in the programme, partly because there were plenty available and partly because goods trains were not glamorous. E. S. Cox, the Chief Designer, an LMS man, was aware of the successful use of 'Black Fives', with their 6ft wheels, on all classes of work, and was convinced that the new 'Britannia' with somewhat smaller wheels would be more generally useful. Moreover, if there was to be any future at all for the freight train, it was going to have to move faster, and the day of the old cart-horse of a goods engine clomping along at 20mph and stopping every few miles to let its bearings cool down was past. Cox favoured a 2-8-2, but R. A. Riddles, who had been responsible for the Ministry of Supply engines, preferred a 2-10-0. This arrangement limited the wheel diameter to 5ft. The RE half-heartedly added 10 engines to the 1953 building orders.

As soon as the '9Fs' started work it was clear that this afterthought was in fact by far the best of the Standards. Before long they were being used as occasional substitutes on passenger turns but the event which really stirred things up took place on 16 August 1958. The engine of the up 'Heart of Midlothian' expired approaching Grantham, particularly bad luck because there was an extra coach-load of assorted Management on the rear. Grantham shed produced a replacement passenger engine by allocating a '9F' to its job, but in their haste the staff mixed it up and shunted the '9F' onto the express. The driver, unconcerned, made up the lost time, going down Stoke Bank at 92mph, but when Management came forward to congratulate him after arrival at King's Cross, its collective jaw dropped when it saw what he was sitting on. The result of course was an immediate 'Thou Shalt Not', but when the corridors of power were convinced that the '9F' had not damaged herself or the track, the practicality of using '9Fs' on fast trains was accepted.

By 1960 the Western Region was using them regularly on Class A trains and considered them for the S&D. They were doubtful about putting such a machine over that curvaceous line at speed but a test run of No 92204 on 29 March 1960 dismissed misgivings as easily as the engine herself dismissed the hills. For the summer timetable four '9Fs' were based at Bath and rostered for the 'Pines'. The first turn was worked by No 92205 and two days later she took a 12-coach 408-ton train through unassisted, despite having part of her brick arch missing. They were duly limited to 410 tons between Bath and Evercreech. Ironically, they were not always used on the 'Pines'; if the load exceeded 410 tons, requiring two engines anyway, it made sense to use a 'West Country' and employ the 'Nine' to dispense with a pilot on another, lighter train.

Below:
On the S&D before the last day of the last season of through expresses, *Evening Star* hauling the 3.40pm Bournemouth-Bath on 18 August 1962, with a curious makeshift device for displaying the train number. Seen crossing the Shepton Montague road half a mile north of Wincanton. *G. A. Richardson*

Above:
The Lickey banker, 'Big Bertha'.
This view was taken in 1926, when
she was converted to burn oil to
beat the miners' strike. *IAL/LPC*

Left:
'9F' No 92079 when she was
Lickey banker, displaying the
badge of office: the electric
headlight (largely ornamental
because stuck up there it was
seldom cleaned). *P. J. Sharpe*

The S&D '9Fs' were:

1960: Nos 92203, 92204, 92205, 92206
1961: Nos 92000, 92001, 92006, 92212
1962: Nos 92001, 92210 (replaced by 92220), 92233, 92245

They were so successful on this job that everyone who ever entered Bath Depot claimed to have suggested it. But they could not be used in winter because they had no train-heating equipment — ludicrous, since it would have been easy to fit (two '8F' 2-8-0s were so equipped for just that purpose). They were not used on freight, because by tradition freight engines went from Bath or Bournemouth to Evercreech or Templecombe, turned round and went back again, and '9Fs' were too long for the turntables at those two places. Thus, now that the Management had to their hands the tool to solve the locomotive problem on the S&D, they failed to use it.

We come at last to the most famous individual engine ever to work the 'Pines': *Evening Star*. She arrived at Bath on 8 August 1962, did several 'Pines' jobs from Saturday 11 August to the last one on 8 September, then departed on the 13th.

Some of the things that happened on the railway in those days were stranger than fiction, and *Evening Star's* career was bizarre. Completed in February 1960, she was allocated to Cardiff (Canton) and alternated between freight work and enthusiasts' tours, for which latter the depot had instructions to polish her up. From September 1962 to August 1963 she was at Oxford. She then went on loan to Bath again, making her last S&D run on the 3.40pm Bournemouth-Bath on 28th September. She received a heavy overhaul at Crewe in February 1963, but by early 1965 was laid aside for exhibition in the hypothetical national transport museum. October 1966 saw her at Crewe awaiting an overhaul which commenced in December and lasted until the next May, then she was parked in Stafford engine shed and was still there in January 1968. Shortly after, she was moved to a store in Brighton. On 2 June 1973 she was transferred to the Keighley & Worth Valley Railway, which restored her to running order. In 1975 she joined the band of steam engines permitted to work on BR (still unable to heat her trains), and toured the country widely. In this era the writer once came to have an unforgettable few minutes driving her — a case of love at first sight convincing me that the '9F' is an engine like no other.

Another '9F' associated with the 'Pines' was No 92079, the Lickey banker. She was allocated to the job when nearly new in May 1956 and remained at Bromsgrove until the end of 1962. When stopped for repairs she was relieved by other engines of the same class from Western Region stock. She is remembered with affection because her short reign covered the formative years of many people who later manned the preservation movement.

From January 1920 to May 1956 the Lickey banker was No 2290, later 22290, later 58100, 'Big Bertha'. This engine was unique as the only one to which the LMS and BR did not apply a power class. It would have been pointless, as although her nominal tractive effort of 43,300lb was higher than any other non-articulated steam engine used in Britain, she was incapable of working a train. With a short wheelbase and four big cylinders fed by only two valves through constricted steam passages, she was strictly a greasy-pole climber. On this job she covered 840,000 miles, representing something like 17 ascents of the bank every working day.

Right:
Driving, old style. Preparing to leave Wolverhampton Low Level on 'Castle' No 7001 *Sir James Milne* with the southbound 'Pines' on 7 May 1963. Use of goggles was most unusual in Britain; indeed, most railways discouraged or forbade it. *IAL*

Right:
Driving, new style. At the controls of a 'Western' class diesel locomotive. *D. Birch*

Far right:
Diesel haulage on the 'Pines', 11 November 1961. BR Type 4 No D103 on the northbound, after stopping in New Street station and before uncoupling. *M. Mensing*

Diesel Haulage

In 1958 the first diesel locomotives suitable for express passenger haulage went into quantity production and were put into the rosters as they came out of the shops, starting with the most important trains and working downwards. By the summer of 1962 most of the regular Bristol-Birmingham line expresses were worked by what were popularly known as 'Peaks': Nos D1-D199, built by BR with English Electric electrical equipment and 2,500hp engines from Sulzer Bros of Switzerland. However, two diesel types particularly associated with the 'Pines' were of the next phase of design.

The Westerns

The rerouteing of 1962 was intended to coincide with full dieselisation of the Western Region Paddington-Birmingham-Birkenhead expresses. Almost as soon as the first diesel-hydraulic locomotives came into use, two major desiderata were adopted for future builds: they should be all-British, and more power was needed. The first 'Western', D1000, was built at Swindon in 1961 and the fleet of 74 was built by Swindon and Crewe in the next three years. The powerplant was two Bristol-Siddeley Maybach MD650 diesel engines, rated at 1,350hp, each driving all three axles of a bogie through a Voith Hydraulic torque converter and a gear and shaft linkage. In common with all the road service locomotives of the period, it carried enough fuel oil for a normal day's work, 800gal. The locomotive weighed 106 tons (against 138 tons for a 'Peak'), with an axle loading of 17tons 13cwt (against 22tons 10cwt for the 'King' steam engine), and with a top speed of 90mph it promised everything the traffic department could want.

The subsequent débâcle happened because the railway put the locomotives to use before they were reliable enough and before there were enough of them to ensure coverage of the rostered work. At one point only 40% of the entire diesel-hydraulic fleet was in working order. As a result steam engines had to be used as substitutes; those were now equally unreliable, for unlike a diesel, a steam engine cannot just be parked down a siding and forgotten until someone wants it. It took another year before the 'Pines' could be booked for diesel haulage with confidence. Meanwhile the British Public, perceiving 'Diesel' as a new-fangled gadget that did not work and 'Steam' as a useless, dirty old relic, voted with its cheque book and bought cars.

The 'Westerns' were soon brought up to scratch but even while they were under construction the new British Railways Board cancelled the diesel-hydraulic programme. By early 1964 the 'Pines' was the only booked 'Western' turn in the Midlands. It was scheduled to end in March but the replacement diesel-electrics also had their troubles and 'Westerns' continued in use for another year.

The Brush Type 4s

In 1959 the Brush Electrical Engineering Co began work on the problem of providing more power, less weight and better reliability than the existing diesel locomotives. This they achieved with a monocoque body structure and a single engine, the Sulzer 12LDA28C of 2,750hp. D1500 was completed in September 1962. So urgent was the demand for locomotives that production orders were already in place, and 512 locomotives were built in just over four years, 312 at the Brush works and 200 at Crewe. The engines were assembled under contract by Vickers of Barrow-in-Furness. The electrical equipment was by Brush, a Type TG160 generator driving six Type TM60 motors.

The Brush Type 4 had an official top speed of 95mph, but was often seen doing the full 100 on the level with 12-coach trains. It was also used on freight trains weighing up to 1,500 tons, in which context it is notable that it was the first British locomotive to have no rail sanding equipment. Despite this lack, D1500 started a load of 690 tons from rest on the Lickey Incline during trials.

The haste to reduce weight and push up the power of the diesel engine came home to roost when in late 1965 they started to suffer from structural cracking, due largely to fatigue and to corrosion in the cooling system. A modification scheme was devised to improve weak spots and alter the balancing of the moving parts; by now there were sufficient locomotives in service for it to be carried out on a rolling programme and the eight locomotives withdrawn for engine changing at any one time did not seriously affect operations. The engines were also governed down to 2,570hp.

Below:
An early diesel appearance on the Stoke route, on 30 September 1959. D214 is hauling five empty coaches, possibly on a test or training run, at Key Green between North Road and Congleton. *M. Mensing*

BR adopted the American philosophy of regarding any machine, however complex, not as a permanent asset but as a consumable for generating profit, and accepted a useful lifespan of 20 years for large diesels. On that basis one would have expected the whole class to be scrapped by 1988, but many were still going strong 10 years later.

Brush Type 4s appeared on the Crewe-Oxford section of the 'Pines' from the spring of 1963 and were the sole power by early 1965. In November 1966, Southern Region drivers were trained on the type in order to eliminate steam haulage on all services running to and from the Western Region. This also took longer than hoped and was not entirely attained until after the 'Pines' finished.

Electric Haulage

From 1960 electric locomotives were used between Crewe and Manchester and Liverpool. However, adoption of electric haulage involves far more than just putting new vehicles on the same rails, and an appraisal of it should include the systems of power generation and transmission, which is beyond the scope of this book.

For the first 25kV overhead electrified lines BR ordered 100 locomotives from Metropolitan-Vickers,

British Thomson-Houston, General Electric Co, English Electric and BR Doncaster Works (the first two were absorbed into Associated Electrical Industries at this time), with the object of testing different designs and components in service. All were designed to the same performance specification, of the same nominal 3,300hp. Towards the end of our period the next generation of locomotives, embodying the conclusions from this experience, was under construction for the much larger Euston-Crewe conversion.

Below:
In New Street on 27 January 1962, an English Electric Type 4 diesel is coupling on to the northbound 'Pines'. The steam blocking the driver's view is leaking from the train heating supply. On the left, BR Type 4 No D135 has brought the train from Bath and is to go forward double-heading on the 'Devonian'. Both locomotives show the curious construction of these classes in which the buffers and couplings are carried on the bogies instead of on the main frame. *M. Mensing*

Above:
Crewe-built Brush
Type 4 No D1587 at
Crewe on 13 May
1964, ready to take
over the
Manchester-
Plymouth. This is
the south end of the
locomotive, carrying
a tail lamp for the
run from the South
depot to the station.
In the background
is a Western
Region 'Warship'
class diesel. *IAL*

Above:
'Western' class diesels worked through to Bournemouth.
This is No D1073 with the 12.15pm from Wolverhampton
on 16 May 1964, heading away from Lymington Junction.
R. A. Panting

On the Line

Portrait of the Pines Express

Carriage Working

A problem that afflicted Manchester, as it did many places, was that when the railway outgrew its town centre station it had to find sites outside the built-up area for such functions as coach storage and servicing; then those sites in turn found themselves hemmed in by building and had to be supplemented by fragmentary facilities wherever a lineside space could be found. In the case of London Road the main depot was at Longsight, 1½ miles out, where there was a locomotive depot and a carriage depot with a large servicing shed. On the Great Central line there were extensive sidings eastward from Ardwick towards Gorton. The 'Pines' remained steam-hauled as it ran empty to and from the sidings for long after its public persona was dieselised, and the last steam working of empty stock to Ardwick ceased at the end of April 1966.

Liverpool had a similar arrangement in the huge complex at Edge Hill, although in this case the origin was different, for it dated from the earliest days when locomotive haulage stopped here and trains were lowered down into the city by ropes.

At Bournemouth the situation was easier, for the carriage yard lay on the east side of the main line between West station and the junctions at Branksome. Trains could be propelled to or from these sidings by their main-line engines without consuming too much of the latter's fuel. Surplus stock could be taken away to sidings at Hamworthy Junction.

Below:
The last steam workings at Manchester Piccadilly were empty stock movements. LMS 2-6-4T No 42343 is at the buffers in the evening of 9 April 1965. Beyond on the left is the side of an electric locomotive showing a cast metal BR emblem. *K. J. Meek*

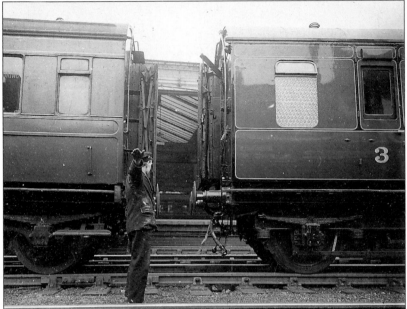

Above:
Coupling up LMS coaches. The photograph bears no other details, although we may deduce from the transverse glass canopy visible that it is in a Midland station. The shunter is waving his hand up and down in the 'Slow Down' signal, prior to raising both hands for 'Stop'. *IAL*

Engine Working

Engine working fell naturally into three parts. A Crewe (North) or, later, Manchester (Longsight) engine worked down to Birmingham. If the formation included Manchester-Birmingham coaches, they were detached together with the engine, which took them away to the sidings at Vauxhall before retiring to Saltley depot to refuel for the return working. A Saltley or Bristol engine went into New Street station and, if the Bradford coaches were running, detached them from their train. When the 'Pines' arrived it coupled on and worked to Bath. In the northbound direction these coaches were uncoupled while the engine was changed at the other end, and then left behind to be collected after the main train had left. This is why the Bradford (or after 1946, Sheffield) coaches were always on the south end of the main train, whereas the Liverpool coaches, which were shunted on by a pilot engine while it stood in Crewe station, were on the north end.

The Liverpool portion was worked to Crewe by an Edge Hill engine, which carried on to Birmingham and in the early years worked the return Liverpool portion back from there. After the Grouping this part of the job was done by a Longsight engine, which worked south from Liverpool in the morning and north to Manchester in the afternoon.

Because of the reversal at Bath it was always necessary to provide another engine facing the other way, which was a principal reason why the S&D remained very much an enclave on its own in motive power matters up to the end of its life. The timings happened to allow the same engine to work the 'Pines' up to Bath in the morning and back in the afternoon. Such an arrangement has the virtue that it allows a depot to keep its best engine on its most prestigious job.

After 1962 London Midland engines worked Manchester/ Liverpool-Crewe (electric) and Crewe-Wolverhampton (diesel or steam), a Western Region engine Wolverhampton-Oxford and a Southern Region engine Oxford-Bournemouth. At first these were based at Longsight, Crewe, Wolverhampton (Stafford Road) and Bournemouth respectively. However, diesel locomotives are not bound to return to a depot at frequent intervals for servicing, as are steam engines, and can roam far between depot visits for examinations every four days. The diesels used on the 'Pines' normally worked right through and were from Crewe or Old Oak Common depots.

Longsight Depot lay on the east side of the main line, just south of Hyde Road. It dated from 1842 but was completely rebuilt several times. There were two engine sheds, the south built in 1870 and north built in 1903, separated from the main line by a carriage shed. They were rebuilt and reduced in size in 1957 and 1948 respectively. In 1934 the LMS modernised the equipment with one of its standard mechanical coaling plants and an ash loader. From 1957 the buildings were progressively turned over to diesel locomotives and trains, and in 1961 a small electric locomotive servicing shed was added. In its heyday in the 1920s the depot was home base to some 250 engines, working all traffic in the area and to London.

One of Longsight's worthy characters was Driver Wilfred Wood, who had the distinction of driving an engine named after himself. He was awarded the Victoria Cross in 1918 for conspicuous bravery in action in Italy and 'Claughton' No 5988 was named *Private W. Wood VC*. The name was transferred to No 6018 and then to the nominal rebuild, 'Patriot' No 5536. Driver Wood retired in 1962, at the same time that his engine was scrapped, and died in 1982.

Locomotive accommodation at Crewe began in 1837 when the Grand Junction Railway chose the station as a refuelling point for its trains, and grew in importance when its maintenance workshops, outgrowing Edge Hill, moved there in 1842. The Steam Shed, as the LNWR called them, stood on the west side

Above:
Through coach manoeuvre in New Street station on 28 October 1961. The Sheffield coaches were detached from the 'Pines' as it stood in Platform 7; now the shunt engine is propelling them along to the release crossovers, seen on the right, where it will draw into the siding. When the northbound 'Devonian' arrives they will move onto its rear. The use of so big an engine as 'Black Five' No 44814 as shunter is not excessive, for she also serves as standby to cover any engine failure, to save time fetching another engine from the shed. *M. Mensing*

Above right:
The next phase of the shunt, on another day, 8 November 1958, with only one coach and a different engine, Midland 4-4-0 No 40443. It is now standing on the middle siding between Platforms 7 and 8, waiting for the Sheffield train. *M. Mensing*

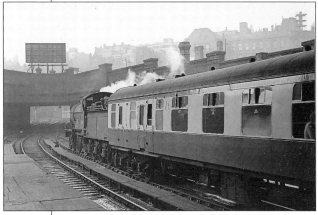

Right:
Attaching the Sheffield coaches to their next train. The photographer noted that this was not the 'Devonian' but a relief which left New Street at 2.45pm on this day, Saturday 4 April 1959. This train always took the through coaches when it ran. The shunting engine is Class 4 2-6-0 No 43049. The shunter is waiting until the movement has come to a stop before he goes between the coaches.
M. Mensing

of the junction at the north end of Crewe station. It was termed the North Depot when the South Depot was built in the yards to the south of the station in 1896. North Depot handled express passenger work and South Depot freight, shunting and local trains. Crewe depots enjoyed tremendous prestige because of course they adjoined the Works and were the first operators of the latest in motive power. Both were rebuilt by the LMS in the 1930s with mechanical coal and ash handling plants. North Shed was on a cramped site which restricted the building to a dead-end shed with 16 roads. It was demolished in 1965 and the site adopted by default as a car park until a signalling control centre was built in it. The South Depot was laid out with plenty of space; engines arriving on shed could refuel, drop their fires and turn, then enter one end of the 12-road shed alongside and in due course emerge from the other end to go off. Steam maintenance came to an end at the close of 1967 and the depot went on to be one of the country's principal diesel locomotive depots.

Saltley Depot lay on the east side of the Midland line by the junction where the New Street link left the direct line, at a lower level than the main line. It also originated in the 1840s, when the Lawley Street site became too crowded to accommodate an engine shed, and the Midland was lucky to find such a convenient spot before Saltley was occupied by industry, particularly rolling stock building firms. Its stabling accommodation was of the roundhouse form with tracks radiating from a central turntable, favoured by the Midland because any engine could be taken out without moving others out of the way. The shed contained three turntables. It was extensively refurbished from 1955 to 1958, but was demolished in 1967. Saltley crews had as wide a working range as any in the country, from Bristol to Carlisle, most of it on freight work.

Bath Depot was on the north side of the line, with the goods yard on the south side, separated from the station by the River Avon. There were two separate depots, a Midland shed built in 1869 on the south side, and one built for the S&D after its extension opened in 1874. They operated independently until the 1930 reorganisation. The original buildings, the Midland a two-road stone shed and the S&D a four-road timber shed, continued in use until final closure in 1966. For most of the time they were adequate, but on summer weekends in the golden years of the 1930s and 1950s, with numerous extra trains coming in, all double-headed and all changing engines, the cramped depot resembled the proverbial pint pot with a quart surging around in it.

One of the peculiarities of the 'Pines' among important expresses was that it was worked by enginemen from a depot with minimal amenities and no allocation of locomotives. This was Branksome, situated inside the triangle of lines outside Bournemouth West station. It had only a small two-road shed and a coal stage which was disused by 1937. After that date it only undertook turn-round servicing of other depots' engines. The engine which its men used to work the 'Pines' to Bath and back made two round trips in the day. Traditionally it worked down from Bath on the 2.40am freight, did the 'Pines' trips and worked back on the 8.10pm freight from Bournemouth. During the summer it would be employed on the overnight Manchester train.

After the 1962 rerouteing Branksome men were given the working to Oxford and back but at the end of 1963 the depot was closed and its staff absorbed into the main depot at Bournemouth Central. No small, élite group likes losing its individuality, although in regarding personal feelings as irrelevant to work BR was no worse than the rest of industry.

Oxford Depot stood on the west side of the line immediately north of the station and opened at the same time as the station in 1850. At that time all operations were on the broad gauge; standard gauge was added in 1854. In 1944 the yard was enlarged by taking over some adjoining sidings. The ageing timber shed saw engines from all parts of the country being serviced, 'West Countries' from Bournemouth standing beside 'B1s' from Nottingham. The depot had the last regular passenger working for a GW engine, the 11am Bournemouth-York, which finished on 3 January 1966, and the shed closed the following day. Diesel locomotive stabling facilities were retained. By then the 'Pines' and others should have been diesel hauled throughout, but the Southern and LM Regions continued to use steam. They were able to carry on engine changing and servicing at Banbury until that depot closed in November. For the last few months, if you took a steam engine north of Basingstoke you were on your own.

The Lickey Incline

Near Blackwell village in the Lickey Hills stood a sanatorium, whose occupants enjoyed a view across the vast expanse of the vale of Severn with, just below their garden, if they appreciated it, the summit of the Lickey Incline.

From the end of Bromsgrove station the line rises 292ft in a distance of 2 miles 7 chains, an average and virtually uniform gradient of 1 in 37.7, to a summit beside some railway cottages just south of Blackwell station. It is a relic of the early railway engineering practice in which lines were laid out like canals, with level stretches where locomotives or horses could be used and the height changes concentrated into rope-worked inclines. By 1835 when it was designed, it was already an obsolete concept and we may assume that the company was more or less cornered into proclaiming that it would work it with locomotives. The first Lickey Banker was built right there in Bromsgrove, the *Great Britain* of 1845. The most famous was the 10-coupled 'Big Bertha' but most of the banking was done by standard Midland 0-6-0 tanks. In January 1957 they were replaced by Great Western '9400' class pannier tanks.

Various observers have chosen to misunderstand the Lickey, saying that there are steeper inclines elsewhere, it is possible to take a run at the ascent, the Midland could easily have built more powerful engines, most engines from the 1930s onwards could have lifted moderate loads up it unaided — all true and all beside the point. What happens elsewhere is seldom relevant in railway operating, for procedures tend to be based on experience at that particular location. The significant feature of the Lickey was that it lay on a main line which

Above left:
At the west end of Birmingham New Street, 'Black Five' No 44919 giving the southbound 'Pines' a good shove under Navigation Street bridge on its way to start the ascent of the BWS line. Steam hangs around to add to the fog on this cold day, 14 January 1961. *M. Mensing*

Left:
A brighter scene at New Street on Thursday 20 June 1957. The southbound 'Pines' has arrived in Platform 7 and 'Black Five' No 44839, with the coaches from Sheffield attached, is backing on to the main train to take it to Bath. The shunter is carrying the thick gloves provided for handling couplings. *M. Mensing*

continued to fall southwards for over 20 miles from the bottom. The presence of an engine placed at the rear of nearly every train was principally to lay the spectre of a breakaway; indeed, bankers were often run on the front of descending trains for the same reason. And Midland engineers would consider it economically quite unsound to provide every Bristol to Birmingham train with at least twice the power that was necessary for all except two miles of its journey; had they lived to see the price-tags on diesel trains which could ascend the incline unassisted, they would have claimed the argument amply proven.

The Midland had a rigid system of train-load control and the use of assisting engines was common and unquestioned; the LMS to a large extent inherited this philosophy. In March 1955, with the need to replace 'Big Bertha' in view, BR ran some tests with 'Black Five' No 44776 hauling seven coaches/222 tons and 'Jubilee' No 45554 *Ontario* hauling eight coaches/252 tons. Both engines proved capable of starting these loads on the incline but the conclusion was that banking should continue as before.

In Midland days the absolute limit for an unassisted ascent was 'Equal to Six vehicles', which meant three postwar bogie coaches. Under BR it was four vehicles or 90 tons, whichever was less.

Lickey Incline Load Limits in tons					
Class of train engine	2	3	4	5	6
Unassisted	90	90	90	90	90
One bank engine	195	215	230	250	270
Two bank engines	295	315	330	350	370

The incline worked like this. Available bankers would stand, not at their shed by the station but on a siding on the up side to the south of the yard, where a coal stage and water column were provided. The load of each train was telegraphed up from Cheltenham to Bromsgrove so that the appropriate bankers were ready. However, if the driver decided he needed more bankers than the table laid down for him, he would whistle approaching Stoke Works signalbox: a short whistle, pause and a number of shorts indicating the number of bankers he wanted. (The 0-10-0 counted as two.) He stopped at a marker 15yd to the rear of Bromsgrove station up home signal, or further up if necessary, to clear the crossover by which the bankers moved onto the back of his train. They were not coupled to the train or to each other. When he was in position each banker gave two crow whistles, and the train driver gave two crows in reply. Then he gave one long whistle and all of them opened their regulators.

At the top the bankers kept pushing through Blackwell station and then shut off and stopped in turn, keeping well apart, then crossed over to the down line

Below:
'Patriot' No 45536 *Private W. Wood, V.C.* standing in the short spur between Platforms 8 and 9, abutting No 2 Signalbox, her fireman enjoying a smoke before he has to get busy again. She is about to take over the northbound 'Pines', which has arrived in Platform 7. The engine from Bath, Class 5 No 73158, is moving off. This view shows a set of LNWR signals still in use but in an appallingly filthy condition; in that place the soot never blows away. The date is 4 April 1959. *M. Mensing*

Above:
Watering the train engine at Evercreech Junction while the assisting engine couples on. The latter, Class 2 No 40569, has a single-line tablet catcher bolted to the tender handrail. The train engine, Class 5 No 73047 borrowed from Bournemouth, does not have one. Taken on Saturday 6 April 1957. *C. P. Boocock*

Right:
Lickey banking on 10 July 1960. No 92079 on the rear of a train of 10 coaches and a van, accelerating through Bromsgrove station onto the incline. The beat of the '9F' working in full gear was thrilling. *IAL*

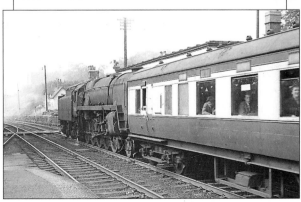

Below right:
The summit of the Lickey at Blackwell. This is on 20 August 1955, before 'Big Bertha's' reign ended, but on this day her place is taken by a new '9F', No 92008. The train is the Saturday 9.15am Weston-super-Mare to Sheffield. Behind the engine are railway cottages (still there in the 1990s) and the sanatorium. *D. Luscombe*

95

and closed up ready to return. To speed things up at busy times, Blackwell down advance starter had a calling-on arm which applied only to the bankers, accepting them down the hill while the station was still occupied. The 'train entering section' signal was given for each engine, even when they were descending together, to make sure they were all accounted for at Bromsgrove. Descending trains were never accepted unless the line was clear as far as Bromsgrove South and were strictly required to slow to 10mph at the top and not exceed 27mph on the way down. Freight trains had to stop at the top to apply wagon brakes and not exceed 11mph.

The Lickey epitomised the steam-worked railway. The labours of the train engine and the bark of the smaller engine behind exuded personality: the 'I can't do it — I will do it' expressed definitively by Wilbert Awdry in his children's stories. Peter Handford, a sound recording engineer, was able to publish his railway recordings on gramophone records, and in the title

Trains in the Hills he captured it in a sequence at Bromsgrove in August 1959. The train is the 'Pines' itself, the engine is Standard Class 5 No 73087 and the bankers are Nos 8405 and 8402. We hear the crow whistles from the bankers, the reply from the train engine, his starting whistle and the explosive bark of the '5' pulling away as hard as possible to get under way in the length of the station before striking the gradient. Then the bankers roar through the station and away into the cutting beyond.

Some writers who like to appear hard-hearted dismiss the Lickey as merely uneconomic and unnecessary but really it was more like the Changing of the Guard at Buckingham Palace: a spectacle of value in itself, one of those things that make life more than pounds, shillings and pence, and even if it was just an entertainment, then the railways owed it to their public. To this day the older inhabitants of Blackwell stroll down to the derelict station on fine afternoons, to sit and remember the show.

The Daily Round

One of the developments attributed to Sir Josiah Stamp was the discovery that the ability of a locomotive to haul a payload was not altered by cleaning the dirt off it, so cleaning was a waste of money. Standard practice was to clean just the cabside numbers so the operating staff could read them. Presumably the public were not interested in what engines looked like; the feelings of the men who had to work with them did not matter — they were not paid to have feelings. All too many pictures of the 'Pines' show the result: a set of smart coaches with a filthy lump of machinery at the front. It backfired on them in the end of course: the squalid look

Below:
Beyond the summit, 0-6-0T No 8409 drops back from the train she has banked.
Brush Electrical Engineering Co

Right:
During the 1955 tests on the Lickey; 'Jubilee' No 45554 *Ontario* nearing the top on a run when she lifted eight coaches unassisted with a start at 30mph through Bromsgrove. The driver clearly has her in full regulator and full gear.
W. A. Camwell

contrasted with the colourful, craftsman-decorated vehicles of the road hauliers, and while British reticence would have prevented potential customers from making comment on this evidence of management attitude, it had its influence on their choices. When Diesel and Electric, came in BR carolled about how bright and clean they were, but by then it was too late.

Carriage cleaning was taken seriously. During the 1930s the LMS equipped its depots with washing plants and vacuum cleaners, and the 'Pines' set could expect to be cleaned every other day.

Coupling up the portions of the train was heavy work. The LMS had no automatic couplings. A shunter had to crouch in the confined space between the vehicles and under the gangway connector in order to lift the vacuum brake hoses off their sealing stoppers and then lift the screw coupling hanging at the coach end over the opposite drawhook. If it did not reach he had to clamber out again to signal the driver to 'Ease up', to push the vehicles more tightly together. He screwed the coupling up so that with the buffers touching it was only just taut. He then coupled the steam heat hoses, turned on their isolating cocks, plugged in the electric lighting control cable and coupled the vacuum brake hoses. An important part of the operation is to uncouple the vacuum hose first when uncoupling, and couple it up last when coupling, to ensure that the brakes remain hard on, unless easing up is required, when you have to place the hose of the front portion on its stopper to allow the driver to move.

Strict adherence to procedure enables it to be done safely. All the same, getting into the middle of several hundred tons of mobile metal gives one a vivid sense of the fragility of the human body.

Readers who are not familiar with this process may see it being carried out on any Heritage Railway.

When any attaching or detaching of coaches had taken place, the guard was responsible for ascertaining that they were in good order, the vacuum brake was working and the red tail lamp was in its proper place.

Steam engines normally need to have their fires cleaned, oiling points replenished and moving parts examined once a day, and their coal capacity is calculated to last the day, but they can carry enough water for only a couple of hours of hard running. When planning engine duties, their endurance must also include time spent collecting and shunting empty stock — such movements when comparatively cold will consume a lot of water — and later on time spent standing in terminal stations before they can be released and moved to a water supply. On the 'Pines' route the Bournemouth-Bath and Bath-Birmingham legs were possible on a tankful of water only with a light load but there was no problem as water could be taken during the booked stops at Evercreech Junction and Cheltenham. Between Manchester and Birmingham, when going via Crewe, the engine could pick up water from the troughs at Whitmore Common. On the Stoke route there was no trough, so a water stop was scheduled. The location varied over the years; before

the war it was at Macclesfield Hibel Road; in postwar summers it was at Kidsgrove Central going south, while going north it was either at Stone or the train stopped on the main line at Grange Junction, north of Etruria and within sight of the famous Shelton Steel Works. Bournemouth-Oxford was another long run; here water could be taken at Basingstoke. There was a trough at Goring between Didcot and Reading but it was no use to the 'West Country' and 'Merchant Navy' class engines as they had no water scoops. When the Bournemouth crews found themselves on GW or LMS engines working this section, they would try the novel game of picking up water, usually getting themselves well damped down in the process.

Two Engines

Except in the low season, the 'Pines' was usually double-headed between Bath and Evercreech Junction, often between Bath and Bournemouth, and sometimes elsewhere. Double-heading was inconvenient, especially for the engine crew who found themselves in the back half of the pair. In tunnels they received the smoke and steam from the front engine in full measure, and even when passing under a bridge the bow wave, bounced down onto their chimney, could interfere with their smokebox vacuum and increase the risk of a blow-back. When the leader picked up water from a trough, the works of their engine would be liberally soused. On the Midland, when double-heading was routine, large plates were fitted in front of the wheels to defend the axleboxes from this spray. Braking was the responsibility of the leading driver, but if the other disagreed with his judgement, or worse, if he interfered, ill-feeling could result. There was no means of communication between them other than by hand signals, or the whistle. When an assisting engine was working in the rear, it was virtually impossible.

As well as on the Lickey, banking took place in Manchester and Liverpool, where the empty stock engine would give the departing train a push out of the platform. On the 1 in 102 incline southwards from Macclesfield to Macclesfield Moss signalbox, banking was provided when needed, although not for ordinary passenger trains. The S&D was famous for double-heading, nearly every through train in summer being assisted over the Mendips between Bath and Evercreech Junction, providing much employment for Templecombe shed. In view of the distance and the running speed required, assisting engines were attached in front, whereas freight trains were usually banked in the rear from Bath or Evercreech to Masbury, the banker returning afterwards. Bankers were also available for the 1 in 60 incline from Poole to Branksome. The Southern often provided 'M7' class tank engines for the job, unwisely, for they were not noted for brisk acceleration. A '9F' with a normal load could easily leave the banker behind. It may seem improbable when contemplated from the comfort of the reader's chair, but on a winter evening in fog or driving rain it was quite possible to lose contact with the train you were pushing without realising it, bringing the risk of a subsequent collision.

For all its difficulties, double-heading and assisting was regarded by the operating and maintenance staff as a good thing, for no one with any sense argues himself out of a job. The real sufferers were the accountants and, indirectly, the fare-payers.

Single Line Working

The Somerset & Dorset was built with a single track. Conversion to double track was undertaken in stages: Evercreech Junction to Templecombe in 1884, Evercreech New to Evercreech Junction in 1886, Radstock to Binegar in 1886, Shepton Mallet to

Left:
On the most difficult but also most beautiful single-line section of the S&D, the southbound 'Pines' entering Combe Down Tunnel on 12 August 1961. The combination is Class 2 No 40564, a regular performer at this time, and 'West Country' No 34045 *Ottery St Mary*. *IAL*

Right:
Combe Down Tunnel seen from the business end of an approaching train. 'Black Five' No 44990, assisted by Midland Class 2 No 40509, on the southbound 'Pines' on 1 June 1949. *H. Weston*

Evercreech New in 1888, Binegar to Shepton Mallet in 1894, Midford to Radstock in 1894 and Blandford to Corfe Mullen in 1905. It was expensive work, involving duplicating bridges and tunnels as the original works had no provision for a second track. This left 26 miles still single; Bath Junction to Midford, Templecombe No 2 Junction to Blandford, and Corfe Mullen Junction to Broadstone, which were never converted.

Control on the single lines was by means of the Tyer electric tablet system. It was extremely safe and reliable; in fact the S&D as a whole was an outstandingly safe railway and suffered no major passenger train accident from 1876 until closure. The original Tyer No 1 instruments installed in 1878 continued in use until 1950. The Templecombe-Blandford section was divided by passing loops at Stalbridge, Sturminster Newton, Shillingstone and Stourpaine. To enable tablets to be exchanged at speed, the Resident Locomotive Engineer, A. H. Whitaker, devised a catcher which was installed in 1904. Attached to the side of the engine, a spring clip held the tablet to be set down and an arm projected to hook the new tablet from a similar clip and arm on a post on the ground. The engine unit was so balanced as to swing upwards when relieved of the weight of the departing tablet. The ground unit was on a pivot, connected by bevel gears to a weighted lever with an overarm movement. The impact of the arriving tablet tripped this lever and swung the unit round so that it was well clear of the passing train. This gadget was said to work at up to 60mph but, even where the track permitted it, drivers would not hit it at that speed

because if it missed, the fireman would have a long walk back. The engine unit was low down on the bunker or tender side, and in order to put tablets on it and take them off the fireman had to climb down the cab steps and hang on with one hand, with his backside well outside the loading gauge. It was appallingly dangerous, yet everyone took it for granted.

Another rural line was the Cheltenham to Southampton route. The through train which conveyed the Liverpool coach was operated by the Great Western, using the engines inherited from the MSWJ and pensioned-off express engines such as 'Barnum' 2-4-0s. In the late 1930s it introduced its '2251' class 0-6-0s. The route was classified 'Restriction Blue', although the larger engines, the '4300', '5100' and '2800' classes, were barred from some sidings because of their width. All these were prohibited south of Red Post Junction for the same reason. At Kimbridge Junction the trains joined the main Salisbury to Southampton line, which could take all but the largest engines.

From Andoversford Junction to Grafton South Junction (near Savernake) was single track, with passing loops at Withington, Foss Cross, Cirencester Watermoor, South Cerney, Cricklade, Swindon Town, Chiseldon, Ogbourne and Marlborough Low Level. From Andover Junction to Kimbridge Junction was single, with passing loops at Andover Town, Fullerton Junction, Stockbridge and Horsebridge. Control was by Tyer electric tablet throughout but there was no high-speed exchanging here.

Left:
Preparing LMS Class 2 No 40568 of Bath depot for duty on 2 June 1954. This engine has a Whitaker tablet changer fitted on the tender. A small part of the wooden engine shed is in the background.
F. J. Saunders

Right:
These two immaculate LMS Class 2s, Nos 600 and 601, ready to take the 'Pines' out of Bournemouth West, both have tablet changers. The photograph is dated August 1936. *G. J. Jefferson*

In 1960 BR introduced numbers comprising the train operating class, an area code letter and a two-digit serial number. The letter for trains crossing region boundaries was O for destinations on the Southern and M for London Midland. The southbound 'Pines' was 1O95, changed to 1O35 after 1962, the northbound was 1M04, and these were kept until 1967. The 9.40am Liverpool-Birmingham was 1G12, the 4.28pm Crewe-Liverpool was 1K29. Western Region steam engines continued to use their number carriers which held only three figures, so they showed O95 or M04; the classification was indicated in the old way by headlamps.

Inexplicably, the S&D persisted in using the headlamp positions which the Midland Railway used at the time of the lease, before it adopted the Railway Clearing House standard: top and left buffer for passenger trains, top and right buffer for freight. It continued to do so until the end, although it will be seen that on the last 'Pines', *Evening Star* carried lamps in the standard positions over the buffers. The Southern, of course, did not use the standard code either but had a six-position code indicating the routeing. In this case, however, through passenger trains passing on and off the Western Region carried standard lamps, or white discs in daylight. 'Pines' pictures show the number 399 on one of the discs; this is the engine duty number for the working from Bournemouth to Oxford and back.

Train Reporting Numbers

From about 1929 the LMSR gave some of its trains identification numbers, shown in the Working Time Table and carried on small boards on the engines. They were applied to long-distance trains or those subject to variations from day to day; the purpose was to assist signalmen and controllers in working them, and in identifying them when they turned up. These numbers were roughly in time order but were not allocated to any rigid system and could change from one timetable to the next. Trains running from the Midland Division to the Western Division (the latter was roughly the southern half of the old LNWR) were prefixed W and those going the other way were prefixed M. Examples of the numbers of the 'Pines' and associated trains are:

Sep 1929:   sb 212, nb 209 to Birmingham, 257 from Birmingham. 9.40am Liverpool-Crewe 376. 12.28pm Bristol-Liverpool 259. 9am Kingswear-Bradford 213.

Jul 1937:   sb 212, nb 244.
9.40am Liverpool-Crewe 376. 10.5am Manchester-Birmingham 214. 8.45am Plymouth- Liverpool 259. 10.20am (SO) Bournemouth-Liverpool 242.

Jun 1947:   sb 220, nb 252. 2.30pm Birmingham-Sheffield 256. 9.55am Bournemouth-Leeds (27 Sep and 4 Oct only) 256.

Jun 1957:   sb 220, nb 236.10.15am Liverpool-Birmingham 62. 10.28am Manchester-Bournemouth 196. 10.30am (SO) Liverpool-Bournemouth 242. 8.0am Plymouth-Liverpool 263. 9.25am (SO) Bournemouth-Liverpool 234. 8.16am (SO) Bournemouth-Liverpool 224. 10.35am (SO) Bournemouth-Manchester Victoria 252.

It will come as no surprise that the S&D used its own numbers. The 'Pines' was typically No 16 or No 17 Down and No 9 Up.

Pathing Problems

Among the namings of 1927 was the 9.45am Liverpool-Euston, which was called the 'London-Merseyside Express', quickly amended to the 'Merseyside Express'. It left Crewe at 10.50, one minute after the 'Pines'. In 1928 it was brought forward to 10.45, so it was about five minutes ahead of the 'Pines' on the run up to Stafford, where they parted company. In the 1930s it was put back to 10.57, so the positions were reversed. Throughout this time it was routed on the fast line, while the 'Pines' ran on the slow line. It would have been more sensible if they had been the other way round, for at Stafford the 'Merseyside' turned left and the 'Pines' turned right. Anyway, if the earlier one was late the two named trains would be racing up the tracks side by side, the driver of the late-running one pushing his engine to make up time and the other man, if he felt like it, keeping up with him for the fun of it.

That was not the only instance of the 'Pines' getting mixed up with another express. On Saturdays in the 1950s the 11.15am from Swansea was booked to stop at Stockport Edgeley at exactly the same time as the northbound 'Pines'. It was put on the slow line but dashed in to London Road in only 10min, while the 'Pines' was booked to take 15 on the fast line. On Saturdays from September 1963, the 9.15am through express from Swansea to Waterloo arrived at Bournemouth Central at 10.4am and left at 10.14. While it was there the 'Pines' came round from the West and ran through on the up centre road without stopping (yet another unique routeing for this idiosyncratic train). The pair ran up through the New Forest with the 'Pines' about 9min in front, then at Southampton the positions were reversed, the 'Pines' stopping while the Swanage passed and went on ahead of it as far as Basingstoke.

The 'Pines' was not even the most important train on the Somerset & Dorset. That position belonged to the 3.40pm Bournemouth-Bath, which carried the mails, connected with the 7.20pm Bristol-Newcastle and was not allowed to be held up by anyone. It crossed with the southbound 'Pines' at Blandford and the latter jolly well had to be there on time. Another feature of postwar working on the S&D was that the little station of Stalbridge had its moment of glory at half-past 10 in the morning. The 8.50am Bournemouth-Bath, making its bucolic way north, shunted clear while the 'Pines', which had started nearly an hour later, overtook it.

Below:
The southbound 'Pines' piloted by '2P' No 40700 with Class 5 No 73050 as train engine. The firemen are taking a breather before the train enters Chilcompton Tunnel south of Midsomer Norton on 19 June 1954. *R. E. Toop*

The Schedules

Portrait of the Pines Express

The examples of timetables shown on the following pages are those presented to the public. The actual route of the train and the times to which it runs are described in the Working Timetable, which is issued to the staff and is far more detailed.

To take the summer of 1937 as an example, there are 44 working times for the Manchester-Bournemouth run, instead of the 12 advertised times. They include the duration of each stop, thus: Stockport 10.10am to 10.12, Crewe 10.41 to 10.49, Wolverhampton 11.39 to 11.41, Walsall (Monday and Friday) 11.49 to 11.54, Birmingham 12.2pm to 12.12, Cheltenham 1.10 to 1.14, Gloucester 1.22 to 1.27, Bath 2.15 to 2.20, Evercreech Junction 3.14 to 3.16, Blandford 4.0 to 4.1 and Poole 4.24 to 4.27. Also specified are passing times at locations which are unknown to the public but are important railway junctions, such as Bushbury Junction north of Wolverhampton, Standish Junction south of Gloucester or Weaver Junction north of Crewe. A large sheaf of Working Timetables was assembled for the preparation of this book.

When looking at them one should bear in mind that the railway was a vast interlocking jigsaw of movement: long-distance passenger trains sharing tracks with freight trains delivering wagons to thousands of stations and factory sidings, mingled with light engines and empty trains running to and from depots. The timings of any one train — for example, a change of a minute in the booked length of a station stop — are what they are because it has to fit together with the movements taking place around it. For instance, it is of little value to coerce firemen to work harder and to invoke a great deal more wear and tear all round in order to get over the Mendips, through Gloucestershire and up the Lickey a few minutes quicker, if the result is to fetch up in New Street at a time when you cannot get into it without altering a large number of other trains and the man who is going to relieve on the engine to take it to shed cannot be there, so an extra man has to be booked on and paid for a shift.

Even the simple railway of the late 20th century can produce some surprises. After the Bournemouth

Left:
Picking up water from Whitmore summit troughs. This view was taken on 16 June 1962, just after the electric equipment had been installed. The train is the 11.20am Euston-Holyhead hauled by 'Patriot' No 45538 *Giggleswick*. The fireman can be seen attending to the scoop handle behind the driver whose hand is on the window sill.
R. J. Farrell

electrification the service pattern on the entire route was largely determined by the Lymington branch, because that was the only remaining single line where the interval between down and up movements was fixed. Times of connecting services were thus also fixed, which in turn decided not only when those must leave from and arrive at Waterloo, but also the paths available for trains coming in from Manchester or Newcastle. Unfortunately, to show the whole picture in all its complexity is beyond the scope of one slim volume.

It is apparent that high speed was not generally a feature of the 'Pines'. The average of 48mph scheduled from Birmingham to Manchester in 1910 was at that time the fastest yet between those cities, but in later years not only did it begin to look rather slow for an express, but the 'Pines' never again reached even that timing. Over the racing ground from Crewe to Stafford, half an hour was the standard time, 49mph. The fastest running was from Bromsgrove to Cheltenham; 36min, 52mph, in 1927 and 33min, 57mph, in 1957. This was a fast time by the standards of the day and pretty demanding for a Class 5 engine hauling 12 coaches. In the diesel era, when far more power was available, several sections were timed at around 55mph.

In the early 1960s the columns of railway magazines, and sometimes of the lay press, were enlivened by a controversy. BR and its publicists eulogised the rise in speeds achieved by its new motive power, permanent way and signalling. Various correspondents responded with vigour that many actual journeys took longer than they had before modernisation or even before the war; not to mention those journeys which were now impossible by train because a particular town had lost its services altogether. It is important to understand that in those days speed of travel was all that interested commentators, and it was taken for granted that it should always increase. Such matters as cost, environmental effect or disturbance to people who were not travelling but had the misfortune to be in the path of those who were, were seldom thought of and never discussed.

In the case of the 'Pines' the accusation of slower travel looks justified. When changes in route are made, or forms of traction are adopted that are as different as motor cars from horses, it is easy to cast doubt on the validity of comparisons. It is true that the numbers of people carried in this train, and in the trains collectively, rose and the standards of comfort improved. But for any one user of the service, what matters is how soon they are delivered to their destination. On that basis, it is reasonable to compare the scheduled times over the route, in whole and between major stations, through the years. Unfortunately, space limitations prevent the detailed analysis from appearing in these pages.

It shows the 'Pines' to be slower after World War 1 than before, and not materially changed during the interwar years. There was an overall slow-down after World War 2 — sensible, for the autumn of 1947 saw the spectacular derailment at Polesworth on the Trent Valley main line when the permanent way disintegrated under a train — although even then the total time from Birmingham to Bournemouth was slightly less than that of 1937.

The change to modern traction made little difference to the northern part of the run, and was in any case nullified by the 1962 switch to a longer route, which added a quarter of an hour. It was claimed at the time that the even longer diversion to Shrewsbury added no time because of the superior speed of diesel traction, but that was true only for the northbound run; southbound it added another quarter of an hour. The slightly longer southern half via Oxford was run in seven minutes less southbound but 19min more northbound. Those who accept the myth that the Somerset & Dorset was 'slow' please note! On this part a really impressive speed-up was effected in the 1963 timetable; remember that the Southern's share of it was achieved with steam. Towards the end of the 'Pines' things were moving a good deal faster on the 25kV electric lines, but otherwise there was no great change.

If one adds to the comparative study the times of the 'Pines' as running when these notes were compiled in 1997, there is no doubt that the travelling is a great deal quicker than in most parts. Not in all, however, — the Birmingham-Manchester time was 1hr 47min in 1997 and 1hr 45min in 1910. We are looking here at a different kind of railway: very few points and crossings, no slow trains, heavier permanent way, realigned tracks and trains with over twice the installed power. Whether it is better or worse than the old kind depends purely on where your interests lie.

The LMS, in common with the other groups, had a habit of printing different, generally earlier, times in its public timetables from those in the Working Time Table. This practice can only be assessed as mischievous. The excuse that it encouraged passengers to be punctual is ludicrous; no one making their way across town to catch a long-distance train is going to cut it so fine deliberately that 2-4min will make the difference between catching it or missing it. Also, if they trouble to note when the train actually starts they will think it is late and regard railway timekeeping as inexcusably sloppy. The fact is that the actual movements of trains formed a vital secret not to be revealed to the public or, if avoidable, to other railwaymen. Working Time Tables and such documents carried the warning, 'The information in this…is Private and must not be given to the Public.' Did the railways think their passengers would desert them if they found out that the train really left Crewe at 10.49 and not 10.45? Or did they imagine there was some rival scheming to purloin the working instructions and put them to some fell purpose? BR had no rivals in the railway field, yet even it held that the sky would fall if, for instance, the public found out that when the fireman of a train in Birmingham New Street station had gone to collect the guard's journal, the driver was permitted to move the engine without him. The explanation can only be that, like all Britons, they just did not want other people to know what they were doing, and wished by releasing the absolute minimum of information to make the life of the passenger (and the subsequent historian) as stressful as possible.

Table 210—
Continued

DERBY, BIRMINGHAM, GLOUCESTER, BRISTOL, and WEST OF ENGLAND

Week Days—Continued

	p.m	a.m	p.m	a.m	p.m	p.m	a.m	a.m	p.m	p.m	p.m	p.m	p.m	p.m	p.m	p.m	p.m	p.m	a.m	a.m
EDINBRO' (Waverley). dep	11 0							9 20	9 20						1210					
GLASGOW (St. Enoch). "	a.m					Saturdays only		9 5	9 5						1032					
BRADFORD (ForsterSq) "	7 35							10 5	10 5						1240					
HARROGATE "	6 22								8 10						10 0					
LEEDS (City) "	8 10								10 10						1215					
NEWCASTLE "	2 4							1125	11 35						1 53					
YORK "	7 258 55														1030					
SHEFFIELD "	9 26 1016														1135				1230	
LIVERPOOL (Central).. "	.. 7 30																			
MANCHESTER(Central) "	7 249 0					1035		11 42						12 6	2 5				1 50	
NOTTINGHAM "	9 21035																			
	a.m	a.m	p.m	a.m	p.m	p.m	a.m	p.m	p.m	p.m	p.m	p.m	p.m	p.m	p.m	p.m	p.m	p.m	a.m	a.m
Derby dep	10 26	1110		..		1145	1222	12 35			1246		1 25	..	2 58	3 15				
Pear Tree and Normanton..	..	..				1156					1253		1 30						51	
Repton and Willington	..	..									1 2		1 39						37	
UTTOXETER dep	..	..											1235						37	
Burton-on-Trent M	10 42	1126				12 4		1275			1 10		1 47	3 15	3 31				7	
Barton and Walton	..										1 20		1 55						4	
Elford	..							New- and Bristol					2 4						13	
Tamworth (High Level)	..	1147				1225		castle to Bristol					2 12						13	
Wilnecote	..					1232							2 18						17	
Kingsbury	..						Saturdays only			To Lichfield (Table 53)			2 25	Saturdays only	Saturdays only				17	
Whitacre	..					1245							2 31						21	
Coleshill	..					1250							2 35							
Water Orton	..												2 41						67	
Castle Bromwich	..																		11	
Saltley	..					1 1														
Birmingham (New St.). arr	11 24	1213				1 8	1 22	1 37					2 55	4 6					11	
LIVERPOOL (Lime St.) dep	8 10			10 25														1140		
MANCHESTER(Lon.Rd) "	8 20			10 20														1135		
LEICESTER (Lon.Rd.). "	10 16										1240									
Birmingham (New St.). dep	11 33		1220	12 42		1 13	1 30	1 44			2 0			York Birmingham						
King's Norton			1234			1 28					2 21									
Northfield		Bradford to Bristol									2 28									
Barnt Green			1244		Dep. Birmingham 12 42 p.m.	1 35					2 36									
Blackwell			1248			1 39					2 40									
Bromsgrove			1255			1 45					2 44									
Stoke Works			1 1	Dep. Birmingham 12 20 p.m.		1 54														
Droitwich Spa			1 8			2 4		2 20			2 58									
Fernhill Heath																				
Worcester (Shrub Hill). arr			1 18			2 14		2 30			3 8									
GREAT MALVERN arr		Sheffield to Bournemouth (forward from Shrub Hill)	2004					3°42			5 15									
HEREFORD "			3 7								5 56									
Worcester (Shrub Hill). dep	..			Manchester (London Road) to Bournemouth		1 25		2 33									4 49			
Wadborough	..					1 35											4 56			
Defford	..					1 42											5 11			
Eckington	..					1 46	Saturdays only										5 17			
Bredon	..					1 52											5Tue			
Ashchurch	..					1 58														
Cleeve	..																			
Cheltenham Spa C. arr	12 29			1 30		2 10		2 27	2 59											
SOUTHAMPTON TER. arr									8 30											
Cheltenham Spa C. dep	12 35	..		1 44		2 17		2 33	3 4								5 47			
Churchdown	..			1 54																
Gloucester arr	12 45			3E°47		2 27		2 43	3 14								5 56			
NEWPORT arr	..							5 38												
CARDIFF (General) "	..			4E°6				6 2												
Gloucester dep	12 53	York to Birmingham	Forward from Worcester at 1 25 p.m.	1 59	2 5		2 49	3 29 3 30	4 0				Except Saturdays			5 45			
Haresfield					2 16				4 11								5 56			
Stonehouse					2 24				4 19								6 11			
Frocester					2 30				4 24											
Coaley					2 35				4 29								6 16			
Berkeley Road					2 41				4 35								6 23			
Charfield G.					2 52				4 45								6 32			
Wickwar					2 58				4 51								6 38			
Yate H.		Derby to Bristol			3 8		Bradford to Bristol		5 1					5 25			6 48			
Mangotsfield					3 17				5 10					5 34			6 54			
270 BATH arr				2 50	4 9			4 25	6 14				6 4			7 42			
272 BOURNEMOUTH WEST "				5 14	7 25			7 25	1044				1044						
Staple Hill					3 22								5 39			7 1			
Fish Ponds					3 26								5 42			7 4			
Bristol (Temple Meads). arr	1 50				3 36		3 45	4 10	5 22				5 50			7 12			
EXETER (St. David's). arr	4 35			7 26			7 26	7 30	8 10				9 19			9 28			
TORQUAY "	6 22								9 36				9 38			1080			
PLYMOUTH (North Rd.) "	6 30								10 5				10 5			1119			

6 October 1947, Table 210. It shows the (then unnamed) 'Pines' in the fourth column and the Sheffield coach in the second column. Old tradition persists; this, being a Midland page, shows a connection from Liverpool Central even though you have to start three hours earlier than from Lime Street! *Author's collection*

105

Table 272 **BATH, TEMPLECOMBE, and BOURNEMOUTH WEST—**
Somerset and Dorset—Southern & L M S

Week Days only

Miles		a.m	a.m		a.m	a.m	p.m		p.m	p.m		p.m	p.m		p.m	p.m	p.m		p.m	p.m		p.m	p.m
	Bath (L.M.S.) ...... dep	..	6 55	..	8 15	10 5	..	..	1 10	..	..	..	2 55	..	..	3 10	4 35	..	4 45	6 0	..	7 0	10 0
4¼	**Midford**	..	7 5	..	8 25	..	..	..	1 20	..	..	..	..	..	..	3 20	..	..	4 55	6 11	..	7 10	1010
6¼	Wellow ....(Halt	..	7 13	..	8 32	..	..	..	1 27	..	..	..	..	..	..	3 27	..	..	5 2	6 19	..	7 18	1018
8¼	Shoscombe & Single Hill	..	7 17	..	8 35	..	..	..	1 30	..	..	..	..	..	..	3 30	..	..	5 5	6 23	..	7 20	1022
10¾	**Radstock A** ..(Welton	..	7 25	..	8 45	1026	..	..	1 38	..	..	..	..	..	..	3 38	..	..	5 13	6 30	..	7 28	1030
12¼	**Midsomer** Norton and	..	7 34	..	8 55	1035	..	..	1 47	..	..	..	..	..	..	3 47	..	..	5 22	6 40	..	7 37	1039
14¾	Chilcompton for D'nside	..	7 43	..	9 3	1043	..	..	1 55	..	..	..	..	..	..	3 56	..	..	5 31	6 48	..	7 46	
17	**Binegar**	..	7 51	..	9 12	..	..	..	2 4	..	..	..	..	..	..	4 4	..	..	5 39	6 56	..	7 54	
18¾	**Masbury Halt**	..	7 55	..	9 17	..	..	..	2 9	..	..	..	..	..	..	4 9	..	..	5 44		..	7 58	
21¾	**Shepton Mallet B**	..	8 5	..	9 26	11 0	..	..	2 17	..	..	from Burnham-on-Sea (Table 273)	..	..	..	4 17	5 22	..	5 52	Except Saturdays	..	8 6	Saturdays only
25	Evercreech New	..	8 11	..	9 33	..	..	..	2 25	..	..		..	..	..	4 25	..	..	5 59		..	8 14	
26¼	Evercreech Junction **C** arr	..	8 16	..	9 39	1110	..	..	2 30	..	..		3 49	..	..	4 30	5 34	..	6 4		..	8 20	
	dep	..	8 18	..	9 42	1112	..	..	2 32	..	..	3 30	3 50	..	..	4 32	5 36	..	6 6		..	8 22	
29¼	Cole **D**	..	8 27	..	9 51	..	..	..	2 40	..	..	..	..	..	..	4 40	..	..	6 13		..	8 36	
33¾	Wincanton	..	8 36	..	1010	1125	..	..	2 50	..	..	..	..	..	..	4 50	5 48	..	6 25		..	8 45	
37	**Templecombe** .... arr	..	8 45	..	1020	1133	..	..	3 0	..	..	3 47	..	..	..	5 0	5 57	..	6 36	..	..	8 55	
	dep	7 25	9 10	..			1220	..	..	3 35	..	..	..	..	4 50	..	6 10	..	..	..	..	9 5	..
38½	**Henstridge**	7 34	9 18	..		..	1228	..	..	..	..	..	..	..	4 58	..	..	..	..	..	..	9 14	..
40¾	**Stalbridge**	7 42	9 23	..		..	1235	..	..	3 45	..	..	..	..	5 5	..	6 19	..	..	..	..	9 20	..
44¼	Sturminster Newton....	8 0	9 32	..		..	1247	..	..	3 53	..	..	..	..	5 16	..	6 27	..	..	..	..	9 28	..
47¾	**Shillingstone F**....(Halt	8 6	9 43	..		..	1255	..	..	4 0	..	..	..	..	5 25	..	6 34	..	..	..	..	9 37	..
50¼	**Stourpaine & Durweston**	8 13	..	..		..	..	..	..	..	..	..	..	..	5 31	..	..	..	..	..	..	Xx	..
52¾	**Blandford**	8 22	9 58	..		..	1 11	..	..	4 12	..	..	4 35	..	5 42	..	6 44	..	..	..	..	9 48	..
54¼	**Charlton Marshall Halt**	8 27	10 3	..		..	1 15	..	..	..	..	..	..	..	5 46	..	..	..	..	..	..	Xx	..
56	**Spetisbury Halt**	8 32	10 8	..		..	1 20	..	..	..	..	..	..	..	5 51	..	..	..	..	..	..	9 55	..
59	**Bailey Gate H**..........	Z8 47	1015	..		..	1 28	..	..	4 25	..	..	..	..	6 0	..	Xx	..	..	..	..	10 2	..
62	Corfe Mullen (E.E.) Halt	..	..	..		..	..	..	..	..	..	..	..	..	..	..	..	..	..	..	..	..	..
63¾	**Broadstone** (Dorset)....	9 0	1034	..		..	1 44	..	..	..	..	..	..	..	6 14	..	7 3	..	..	..	..	1015	..
65	Creekmoor Halt	9 5	1039	..		..	1 49	..	..	..	..	..	..	..	6 18	..	..	..	..	..	..	1021	..
67	**Poole**	9 10	1044	..		..	1 55	..	..	..	..	..	5 2	..	6 23	..	7 12	..	..	..	..	1026	..
69	Parkstone	9 19	1052	..		..	2 3	..	..	..	..	..	..	..	..	..	..	..	..	..	..	1032	..
70¾	**Branksome**	9 24	1058	..		..	2 8	..	..	..	..	..	..	..	..	..	..	..	..	..	..	1038	..
71¾	**Bournemouth West** arr	9 30	11 3	..		..	2 13	..	..	..	..	..	5 14	..	6 35	..	7 25	..	..	..	..	1044	..

Table 273 **BURNHAM-ON-SEA, BRIDGWATER, WELLS, GLASTONBURY AND STREET, and EVERCREECH JUNCTION**—Somerset and Dorset—Southern & L M S

Week Days only

Miles		a.m	a.m	a.m		a.m	a.m	p.m		p.m	p.m	p.m		p.m	p.m	p.m		p.m	p.m		p.m	p.m	
	Burnham-on-Sea ...dep	..	..	..	..	9 30	1130	..	..	2 15	2 40	..	..	4 0	..	..	..	6 0	..	..	6 45	7 40	..
1½	**Highbridge A** .... arr	..	..	..	..	9 35	1135	..	..	2 20	2 45	..	..	4 5	..	..	..	6 5	..	..	6 50	7 45	..
	dep	7 0	..	..	..	9 53	..	..	..	2 23	..	..	..	4 8	..	..	..	..	..	..	6 57	..	..
3¾	Bason Bridge............	7 4	..	..	..	9 58	..	..	..	2 29	..	..	..	4 14	..	..	..	..	..	..	7 4	..	..
6¾	Edington Junction ..arr	7 11	..	..	..	10 6	..	..	..	2 36	..	..	..	4 20	..	..	..	..	..	..	7 11	..	..
—	**Edington Junc.** dep	..	8 22	..	..	1010	..	..	..	2 40	..	..	..	..	..	5 28	..	..	..	..	7 20	..	..
9¾	Cossington	..	8 30	..	..	1015	..	..	..	2 50	..	..	..	..	..	5 33	..	..	..	..	7 25	..	..
11	Bawdrip Halt	..	8 35	..	..	1020	..	..	..	2 55	..	..	..	..	..	5 38	..	..	..	..	7 30	..	..
14	**Bridgwater** .. arr	..	8 45	..	..	1028	..	..	..	3 5	..	..	..	..	..	5 46	..	..	..	..	7 38	..	..
— Mls	**Bridgwater** ..dep	..	..	..	..	9 40	..	..	..	2 10	..	3 55	..	..	..	..	..	..	6 40	..	..	..	..
— 3	Bawdrip Halt............	..	..	..	..	9 47	..	..	..	2 15	..	4 0	..	..	..	..	..	..	6 45	..	..	..	..
— 4½	Cossington	..	..	..	..	9 52	..	..	..	2 20	..	4 5	..	..	..	..	..	..	6 50	..	..	..	..
— 7½	**Edington Junc.** arr	..	..	..	..	10 0	..	..	..	2 28	..	4 13	..	..	..	..	..	..	6 56	..	..	..	..
—	Edington Junction.. dep	7 12	..	..	..	10 7	..	..	..	2 37	..	..	..	4 21	..	..	..	..	..	..	7 12	..	..
9	Shapwick **J**	7 18	..	..	..	1013	..	..	..	2 43	..	..	..	4 28	..	..	..	..	..	..	7 19	..	..
11	Ashcott **K**...............	7 22	..	..	..	1018	..	..	..	2 47	..	..	..	4 33	..	..	..	..	..	..	7 23	..	..
13½	**Glastonbury & Street** arr	7 30	..	..	..	1025	..	..	..	2 55	..	..	..	4 40	..	..	..	..	..	..	7 31	..	..
—	**Glastonbury G** dep	..	..	9 30	..	1040	..	..	..	..	..	..	..	..	5 10	..	..	..	..	..	7 45	..	..
16¾	**Polsham Halt**..........	..	..	9 38	..	1045	..	..	..	..	..	..	..	..	5 18	..	..	..	..	..	7 50	..	..
19¾	**Wells L**........ arr	..	..	9 48	..	1054	..	..	..	..	..	..	..	..	5 26	..	..	..	..	..	7 59	..	..
— Mls	**Wells L**........ dep	..	..	..	..	1010	..	1 30	..	..	..	..	..	4 25	..	..	..	..	..	..	7 15	..	..
— 2¾	**Polsham Halt**	..	..	..	..	1015	..	1 35	..	..	..	..	..	4 30	..	..	..	..	..	..	7 20	..	..
— 5¾	**Glastonbury G** arr	..	..	..	..	1023	..	1 43	..	..	..	..	..	4 38	..	..	..	..	..	..	7 28	..	..
—	**Glastonbury & Street** dep	7 33	..	..	..	1028	..	..	..	2 58	..	..	..	4 43	..	..	..	..	..	..	7 37	..	..
19	**West Pennard**	7 44	..	..	..	1039	..	..	..	3 9	..	..	..	4 54	..	..	..	..	..	..	7 49	..	..
22¼	**Pylle**	7 54	..	..	..	1050	..	..	..	3 18	..	..	..	5 5	..	..	..	..	..	..	7 56	..	..
24	**Evercreech Junc. C** arr	8 0	..	..	..	1056	..	..	..	3 25	..	..	..	5 11	..	..	..	..	..	..	8 5	..	..

A Adjoining G.W. Station
B Charlton Road
C Station for Castle Cary (3 miles)
D Station for Bruton (1½ miles). and Castle Cary (2 miles)
F Station for Child Okeford (1 mile) and Okeford Fitzpaine (1¼ miles)
G Glastonbury and Street
H Station for Sturminster Marshall
J Station for Westhay (1 mile)
K Station for Meare (1½ miles)
L Priory Road
m Third class only
■ Through Carriages
Z Arr 8 39 a.m
Xx Stops to set down on notice to Guard

6 October 1947, Tables 272 and 273, the S&D. Note that only four trains ran the whole length of the line, one of them the 'Pines'. In those days 'Week Days only' included Saturdays, so it means that the S&D was closed on Sundays.

The Pines Express

AND OTHER
THROUGH EXPRESS TRAINS

between

MANCHESTER, LIVERPOOL

and

CHELTENHAM, GLOUCESTER, BATH, BOURNEMOUTH

WEEKDAYS ONLY

NORTH TO SOUTH

		SX am	SX am	SO am	SO am	SO am	SO am	SO am	PO
Manchester London Road	dep	....	10 15	10 20		10 28		10 28	
Stockport Edgeley	,,	....	10 27	10 33		10 41		10 41	
Liverpool Lime Street	,,	10 15	....		10 30		10 30		
Crewe	,,		11 12		11 30	11 35	11 30		
Birmingham New Street	,,		pm 12 40						1 20
				pm		pm	pm	pm	
Cheltenham Spa Lansdown	arr	1 39		2 7	2 32	2 53	2 32		
Gloucester Eastgate	,,	1 58		2 23			3 52		
Bath, Green Park	,,	3 0		3 25	3 52	4 15	5 7		
Shepton Mallet Charlton Rd.	,,					5 7	5 18		
Evercreech Junction	,,	4 2		4 26	4 53	5 18	6 46		
Blandford Forum	,,	4 53		5 20	5 38	6 40	6 59		
Broadstone	,,	5 12		5 43	5 58	6 59	7 9		
Poole	,,	5 20		5 53	6 8	7 9	7 23		
Bournemouth West	,,	5 32		6 8	6 23	7 23			

SOUTH TO NORTH

		SO am		SO am	SX am	SO am	SO
Bournemouth West	dep	8 16		9*25	9 45	9†45	10 35
Farkstone	,,			9 36			
Poole	,,	8 24		9 44	9 54	9 54	10 44
Blandford Forum	,,				10 20	10 20	
Sturminster Newton	,,				10 38		
Stalbridge	,,						
Wincanton	,,						
Evercreech Junction	,,	9 34		10 50	11 2	11 4	
Shepton Mallet Charlton Rd.	,,				11 18		
Bath, Green Park	,,	10 45		11 50	12 1	12 5	
				pm			
Gloucester Eastgate	,,	11 53		1 0	12 57	1 15	
Cheltenham Spa Lansdown	,,	12 14		1 20	1 16		
		pm					
Birmingham New Street	arr	1 21			2 25		
Crewe	,,	2 57		3 47	3 41		
Hartford	,,			4 10	4 10		
Runcorn	,,	3 32		4 28	4 28		
Liverpool Lime Street	,,	3 54		4 50	4 50		
Wilmslow	,,				4 17		
Stockport Edgeley	,,			4 46	4 32	5 24	
Manchester London Road	,,			5 5	4c45	5 40	

*—Seats reservable to Liverpool and Manchester only. †—Seats reservable to Manchester only. A—Via Stoke-on-Trent
(depart 11.55 pm). FO—Fridays only. SX—Saturdays excepted. SO—Saturdays only. c—Manchester Mayfield.
d—Manchester Victoria.

Seats on these trains can be reserved in advance
from Manchester, Liverpool and Bournemouth
on payment of a fee of 1s. 0d. per seat.

17 June to 15 September 1957,
the summary page. *Author's collection*

THE PINES EXPRESS

AND OTHER

THROUGH EXPRESS TRAINS

BETWEEN

MANCHESTER, LIVERPOOL

AND

BATH, BOURNEMOUTH WEST

WEEK DAYS ONLY

NORTH TO SOUTH

		MONDAYS TO FRIDAYS "THE PINES EXPRESS" Restaurant Car Train Manchester to Bournemouth Through Carriages from Liverpool		SATURDAYS ONLY "THE PINES EXPRESS" Restaurant Car Train Manchester to Bournemouth		SATURDAYS ONLY Through Train Liverpool to Bournemouth Through Carriages from Manchester		FRIDAYS ONLY 29th June to 17th August Through Train Manchester to Bour.	
Manchester ⌠(Piccadilly) .. dep		am 10A30	..	am 10A25	..	am 10A55	..	pm 10A20 10A50	..
⌡(Central) ...... "									
Stockport (Edgeley) .. "		10 41		10 38		11 7			
Liverpool (Lime Street) .. "		10A15				10A30			
Crewe .. .. — "		11 19				11 40			
Birmingham (New Street) .. "		12 45						11A24	
Bath Green Park .... arr		pm 3 3	..	pm 3 25	..	pm 3 55	..	pm 3A45	..
Shepton Mallet (Charlton Road) "						5 8			
Evercreech Junction ...... "		4 5		4 26		5 18			
Wincanton .... "						5 30			
Templecombe .... "				4 55		5 38			
Stalbridge.. .. .. .. "						5 56			
Sturminster Newton .... "						6 3			
Shillingstone .... "						6 13			
Blandford Forum .... "		4 53				6 20			
Broadstone .. .. .. "		5 12		5 20		6 42			
Poole .... "		5 20		5 43		6 53		6B31	
Bournemouth West .. "		5 32		5 55		7 5		6B44	
					6 8				

SOUTH TO NORTH

		SATURDAYS ONLY Through Train Bournemouth to Liverpool Through Carriages to Manchester		MONDAYS TO FRIDAYS "THE PINES EXPRESS" Restaurant Car Train Bournemouth to Manchester Through Carriages to Liverpool		SATURDAYS ONLY "THE PINES EXPRESS" Restaurant Car Train Bournemouth to Manchester		SATURDAYS ONLY 30th June to 25th August Through Train Bournemouth to Manchester	
Bournemouth West .. .. dep		am 9C25	..	am 9A45	..	am 9A45	..	am 10A32	..
Parkstone .... "		9 32						10 41	
Poole .... "		9 39		9 54		9 54		11 11	
Blandford Forum .... "		10 7		10 19		10 19		11 11	
Sturminster Newton .... "								11 36	
Stalbridge .... "				10 40				11 36	
Wincanton .... "								12 5	
Evercreech Junction ...... "		10 52		11 6		11		12 12	
Shepton Mallet (Charlton Road) "				11 18					
Bath Green Park .... "		11 50		pm 12 1		pm 12 5		pm 1	
		pm							
Birmingham (New Street) .. arr				2 18				3 53	
Crewe .. .. "		3 55		3 43				3 54	
Hartford .. .. "		4 17		4 9				6B25	
Runcorn .. .. .. "		4 28		4 20				6B40	
Liverpool (Lime Street) .. "		4 49		4 16				6B31	
Wilmslow .. .. .. "		4 37							
Stockport Edgeley ... .. "		4 47		4 25		5 25		6 18	
Manchester ⌠(Piccadilly) .... "		5 1		4 38		5 40		6 47	
⌡(Victoria) "									

Seats may be reserved at a fee of 2/- per seat upon personal or postal request to the Station Master. Early application is advisable	B Change at Crewe C Seats reservable to Liverpool and Manchester only. "See Note A" D Seats reservable to Manchester only. "See Note A"	F Tiviot Dale Station p pm S Saturday morning

18 June to 9 September 1962, the summary
page in the Southern Region timetable.
Author's collection

THE PINES EXPRESS

RESTAURANT CAR SERVICE

MANCHESTER, LIVERPOOL, WOLVERHAMPTON, BIRMINGHAM, LEAMINGTON SPA, SOUTHAMPTON and BOURNEMOUTH

VIA OXFORD and BASINGSTOKE

From NORTH to SOUTH—WEEK DAYS ONLY

				am	
Manchester (Piccadilly)	.. .. ..	dep	..	10A 0	..
Stockport (Edgeley)	....	,,	..	10 11	..
Liverpool (Lime Street)	.. .. ..	,,	....	9 48	...
Crewe	.. .. ..	,,	....	10 55	...
Shrewsbury		,,	..	11 35	..
Wellington		,,	..	11 54	..
				pm	
WOLVERHAMPTON (Low Level)	.. .. ..	dep	..	12 21	..
BIRMINGHAM (Snow Hill)	....	,,	......	12 44	....
Leamington Spa General		,,	......	1 9	....
Oxford		,,	......	2 4	....
Reading West	.. .. ..	,,	......	2 46	....
Basingstoke		arr	......	3 8	....
Winchester City	.. .. .. A ..	,,	......	3 34	....
SOUTHAMPTON CENTRAL	....	,,	......	3 52	....
West Cowes Pier		arr	......	40 5	....
BOURNEMOUTH CENTRAL	.............arr		......	4 32	....
,, WEST		,,	..	4 44	..

From SOUTH to NORTH—WEEK DAYS ONLY

				am	
BOURNEMOUTH WEST	.. ..	dep	..	10A 0	..
,, CENTRAL	....	,,	..	10A 10	..
West Cowes Pier	.. ..	dep	..	90 5	..
SOUTHAMPTON CENTRAL	....	dep	......	10 45	......
Winchester City	.. ..	,,	......	11 8	......
Basingstoke	....	,,	......	11 40	......
				pm	
Reading West	.. .. ..	arr	..	12 6	....
Oxford	....	,,	....	12 48	....
Banbury	....	,,	....	1 29	....
Leamington Spa General		,,	....	1 52	....
BIRMINGHAM (Snow Hill)	.. .. ..	,,	....	2 27	....
WOLVERHAMPTON (Low Level)	....	,,	....	2 52	....
Wellington	.. .. ..	,,	....	3 14	....
Shrewsbury	....	,,	....	3 30	....
Crewe	.. .. ..	,,	....	4 14	....
Hartford	....	,,	....	4 41	....
Runcorn..	....	,,	....	4 55	....
Liverpool (Lime Street)	....	,,	....	5 17	....
Wilmslow	....	,,	..	4 51	....
Stockport (Edgeley)	....	,,	..	4 59	....
Manchester (Piccadilly)	....	,,	..	5 12	..

A Seats can be reserved in advance on payment of a fee of 2s. 0d. per seat	B Subject to alteration commencing 1st January, 1964	0 Calls to take up passengers only

9 September 1963 to 14 June 1964, the summmary
page. West Cowes Pier is on the Isle of Wight, by boat
and a longish walk from Southampton. *Author's collection*

8

'Pines' Flourish Again

Portrait of the Pines Express

The wholesale service withdrawals of 1967 were in accord with the policy of the time; BR was in business to run regular shuttles between London and other major cities, and was not interested in any seasonal traffic or anything that threaded irregularly across the main routes. This is understandable, as far as it goes — most readers of these notes would prefer a simple pattern of work and a regular income.

Twenty years later, however, the scene had changed again. The relative decline of London was continuing and had to be recognised; South Coast towns were growing explosively and were now major commercial enclaves; the disappearance of slow freight and local trains permitted much faster running on journeys which had traditionally been counted unattractive on the score of time. The upshot of this new climate was a new 'Pines Express' in 1992. Its timings are included in some of the tables, but the comparison is barely valid, for it was a very different animal from the old one.

It adopted yet another route permutation. From Manchester it reverted to the Potteries route, via Cheadle Hulme, Stoke and Norton Bridge, but this time there was no nonsense of not stopping at Stoke, which since full electrification had gained decent long-distance services for the first time. It called at Macclesfield and Stafford, places formerly scorned by through trains, and thence to Wolverhampton High Level and Birmingham New Street.

Below:
It is impossible to discern any pride in service in this view during the low years at Mortimer on the Reading-Basingstoke line; untended, a playground for local urchins, furnishings stripped and replaced by items whose only criterion is cheapness. Brush Type 4 diesel No 47328 appears with the post-'Pines': the Saturday 09.10 Manchester-Poole. *J. C. Baker*

	M-S	M-S
Manchester Picc	d 08.17	a 19.33
Stockport	08.24	19.19
Macclesfield	08.37	19.02
Stoke	a 08.57: d 08.58	18.42
Stafford	09.19	a 18.21
Wolverhampton	09.35	a 18.05: d 18.06
Birmingham NS	a 09.54: d 10.06	a 17.40: d 17.46
Birmingham Int	d 10.16	17.25
Coventry	10.27	17.12
Leamington Spa	10.44	16.58
Banbury	a 11.03	16.39
Oxford	11.24	16.16
Reading	a 11.54: d 12.02	a 15.44: d 15.50
Basingstoke	a 12.28: d 12.29	a 15.24: d 15.25
Winchester	a 12.44: d 12.45	15.08
Southampton Airport	a 12.53: d 12.54	d 14.58
Southampton Central	a 13.01: d 13.05	a 14.49: d 14.50
Brockenhurst	a 13.18: d 13.19	a 14.35: d 14.36
Bournemouth	a 13.40	d 14.21

From Birmingham it proceeded to Coventry and turned right onto a link line to Leamington Spa, which had been closed to passenger trains but was rebuilt in 1977 to provide an alternative route for the growing number of passenger trains on the once-despised GW main line. At Reading it went into the General station and reversed, to continue to Basingstoke and down to Bournemouth. It did not serve Poole but went from Bournemouth into Branksome carriage depot for servicing.

It stopped at two new stations: Birmingham International, between Marston Green and Hampton in Arden, serving Elmdon Airport; and Southampton Airport, between Eastleigh and Swaythling. (Eastleigh was the airfield from where the Supermarine Spitfire first flew, thus the new 'Pines Express' could now be dubbed a 'Battle Of Britain Memorial Express' as it passed the birthplaces of the Lancaster and Spitfire.)

The train itself was now an HST, a permanently coupled set with a diesel locomotive at each end, and over a new, simplified railway with heavier track its two Paxman Valenta 2,250hp marine diesel engines could knock over an hour off the previous best journey time. One train could now make the round trip in the day, with a 40min turnround. Although as the 1997 timetable shows, the modern Mancunian must get to Piccadilly station for an 8.17am departure, early starts are more popular than they used to be. Liverpool passengers are less well served, their only through train being a 15.10 Liverpool-Poole and an 06.42 Poole-Liverpool.

If the new 'Pines' is flourishing, what of the old? It was remembered in Radstock, where a housing development on the site of the railway carries the street names 'Pines Court' and 'Pines Way'. There is another 'Pines Way' in Bath, on the site of the goods depot, together with a 'Stanier Road' and 'Ivo Peters Road', the latter named after an enthusiast who spent a lot of time photographing S&D trains. The Bournemouth-Poole conurbation has spread, housing and factory estates have swallowed up Broadstone and beyond, and rush-hour traffic streams out to Wimborne and Blandford.

In the midst of all this the S&D has sunk back into the fields and is one with the Roman roads and villas. The only people wishing to preserve its memory were the railway enthusiasts. The Somerset & Dorset Railway Museum Trust was formed with a view to restoring part of the line, and established a base at Radstock engine shed, but was driven out by local opposition. In 1975 the Trust looked for a site where it could house its collection of S&D relics and was offered a home at Washford station on the West Somerset Railway. Here a new museum has been built on the site of the goods depot, and wagons, coach bodies, the signalbox from Burnham-on-Sea and the goods office from Wells are on display. The most spectacular item is S&D 2-8-0 No 88, which runs on the railway; but it should be remembered that she has no direct connection with the 'Pines'.

The explorer who would wish to re-create the experience of riding in an LMS train may do so on the Severn Valley Railway, from Kidderminster to Bridgnorth, or at the Midland Railway Centre at Butterley in Derbyshire. There are also LMS coaches at the Scottish Railway Preservation Society's railway at Bo'ness on the Firth of Forth. The number of preserved locomotives associated with the 'Pines' is felicitously large and includes examples of all the types and classes, but for a major exception. There is not one Midland Railway 4-4-0, apart from No 1000 which is not typical of the type; nor one of the LMS version; nor, for that matter, one from the LNWR or many other railways. This lack is not, of course, to be laid at the door of the preservation movement, which lost many such locomotives through lack of resources, but arose because there were not enough interested and influential people around at the time to prevent it. As we approach the end of the century, thoughts are turning to the idea of making good the deficiency by building new locomotives to the original designs, and these projects deserve support. The real thing is just as real even if it is not a hundred years old.

Setting up modern-day reconstructions is fine as long as those responsible do not make false claims of authenticity. No Heritage Railway can take passengers on board a 12-coach train for seven hours (or can they? — there's a challenge!) but that does not stop them paying tribute in whatever way they can. It would be quite appropriate to run a 'Salute to the Pines' behind a Class 4F 0-6-0 or even an LMS Class 4 2-6-0; better, if one wants a headboard, to use a 'Castle', one of the few classes to carry a headboard on the actual train; most prototypical, however, will be a dirty 'Black Five' with no headboard.

Such is the march of time that a 'Western' class diesel hauling a set of BR Mk 1 Standard coaches is a historical relic of the 1960s not found on the commercial railway, and its devotees are equally keen to preserve it. Such a train may also be found on the Severn Valley Railway. In 50 years the conservation of artefacts (and this does not just apply to railway trains, of course) has become better organised and has profited from the experiences of the pioneers. No doubt we shall, in due time, see a 'Nostalgic Pines Express' being run by a preserved High Speed Train, with enthusiastic volunteers in period uniforms staffing the buffet car.

The railway influence on Bournemouth was profound. You will still hear Lancashire and Yorkshire voices on the promenade. In 1997 the writer visited a guest-house near where the West station once was, and found, on this random dip into the resort, fellow visitors from Birmingham and Nottingham who had arrived by train, following the pattern set by the Midland Railway all those years ago. The pines, seeded in the 1860s, grew to fruition in the 1920s and were cut down in the 1960s, but new pines are growing in the 1990s and may stand in the sun to welcome generations to come.

Above:
The northbound 14.21 'Pines Express' for Manchester Piccadilly departs from Bournemouth on 3 February 1997. *Brian Morrison*

Left:
Basingstoke on 7 April 1995, No 43013 (once *University of Bristol*) powers the rear of the 14.21 Bournemouth-Manchester Piccadilly HST, while No 43100 *Craigentinny* (right) restarts from the station heading the 06.50 service from Edinburgh to Bournemouth.
Brian Morrison